MW00532784

THE
LITTLE
BOOK
OF
DEATH

NEIL R. STOREY

To Andrew, my dear friend, fellow
ghost-hunter and collector of
antiquarian books of the eerie, the
horrible and the strange.

First published 2013

The History Press
The Mill, Brimscombe Port
Stroud, Gloucestershire, GL5 2QG
www.thehistorypress.co.uk

British Library Cataloguing in Publication Data.
A catalogue record for this book is available from the British Library.

ISBN 978 0 7524 7151 8

Typesetting and origination by The History Press
Printed in Great Britain
Manufacturing managed by Jellyfish Solutions Ltd

CONTENTS

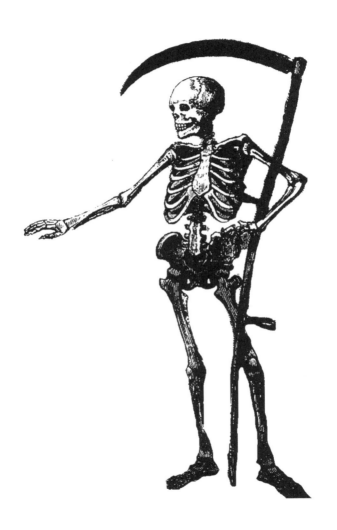

INTRODUCTION

'There is nothing certain in life but death and taxes.'

Benjamin Franklin, 1789

This little book is a repository of intriguing, fascinating, obscure, strange and entertaining facts and trivia about the one certainty in all our lives – death. Within this volume are some horrible, unfortunate and downright ludicrous ends.

Find out what body parts of the departed – be they great, famous or infamous – are still with us. Learn of portends of death, odd last requests, burials, epitaphs and death rites, as well as the strange fates of some cadavers – for here be mummies, incorruptibles, bog people, auto-icons – and even the frozen dead. Anyone curious or morbid enough to enjoy this macabre miscellany will be entertained and enthralled and never short of some frivolous fact to enliven conversation or quiz.

I hope you'll find in this book many things that you did not know you wanted to know about death and the dead – until now…

Neil Storey, 2013

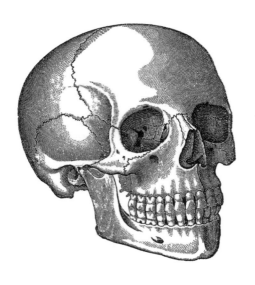

1

WHAT A
WAY TO GO!

In 1856, unfortunate East Sussex resident Matthew Gladman entered the Lewes High Street water closet after dark, unaware that the floorboards had been removed for cleaning. He fell into the cess pit and died of asphyxiation by methane gas.

Lord Palmerston, twice Prime Minister of Great Britain, died of a heart attack while having sex with a young parlourmaid on his billiard table on 18 October 1865.

Jazz trumpeter Joe 'Poolie' Newman was always known as a ladies' man. In 1989, Newman determined to maintain his reputation with a penile implant. All seemed to go well – until, during a visit to a restaurant, a build-up of pressure caused his member to explode. He bled to death.

In 1984, Jimmy Fixx, the man credited with starting the jogging craze, died of a heart attack at the age of fifty-two, shortly after his return from his daily run.

Radium pioneer and double Nobel Prize winner Marie Curie died, in 1934, from aplastic anaemia contracted due to her long-term exposure to radiation.

Mr Walter Morgan of Morgan's Brewery on King Street, Norwich, met his death by falling into a vat of beer in May 1845.

Jasper Newton 'Jack' Daniel, founder of Jack Daniel's Tennessee Whiskey Distillery, died from blood poisoning in 1911 after a run-in with his safe: he forgot the combination and kicked it, cutting his toe. The wound became infected, and killed him shortly afterwards.

A wedding-party guest in South Carolina, USA, was killed in 1992 when he was struck by the aircraft carrying the bride and groom as he mooned at them from the runway.

Distinguished mountaineer Gerard Hommel, a veteran of six Everest expeditions, died after falling off a ladder: he slipped and cracked his head on a sink as he was attempting to change a light bulb in the kitchen of his home in Nantes, France, in 1993.

In August 1848 Thomas Ireson thought it would be a good idea to tie himself to the tail of a cow at Mattishall in Norfolk. The infuriated animal kicked him to death.

A seventy-two-year-old grandmother from Birmingham was delighted to accept a jelly sweet from her two-year-old great-grandson in 1992. However, he then pulled off his hat to reveal a new short hair do: the poor lady found the new haircut so hilarious that she burst into uncontrollable laughter and choked to death on the sweet.

Internationally renowned escapologist Harry Houdini proudly claimed he could withstand any blow to the stomach. However, when he was challenged by McGill University student J. Gordon Whitehead in Montreal in 1926 he did not have time to prepare himself to receive the blow. He died of acute peritonitis caused by a ruptured appendix.

A sixty-two-year-old man living in East Sandwich, Massachusetts, was found dead from carbon-monoxide poisoning in his home in 2008: a racoon had died in the chimney flue and blocked it, allowing poisonous gases to build up.

George Conklin, one of the keepers for Barnum's show at Olympia in London in 1889, was going about his daily business of cleaning out the animals when he heard a cry of, 'Take him away!' It was coming from another stall. Rushing over, he saw two elephants standing together. He seized a broom and set about separating them, and, as he did so, he spotted fellow keeper George Stevens sitting up against the wall in a crouching position; blood was coming from Stevens' mouth. The injured man died moments later. The inquest concluded he had perished after being sat on by an elephant.

Street vendor Igor Roskny of Perth, Australia, was beaten to death by an irate customer in 1994 after he mistakenly put mustard on the customer's tuna sandwich. The murderer argued he had clearly stated that he wanted mayonnaise.

Jamie Ward was enjoying a relaxing time sunbathing at Leland, North Carolina, in August 2008 when a pool umbrella broke loose and impaled his head, killing him instantly.

On 15 January 1919, a huge storage tank of molasses blew up: 2.3 million gallons of molasses were sent careering down the streets of Boston, Massachusetts, in a 30ft tidal wave, leaving twenty-one people dead and 150 injured.

In June 2003, New Jersey landscaper Rigoberto Martinez kicked a tree branch to force it into a wood chipper. Tragically, he was pulled into the shredder with it and received fatal injuries.

French President Félix François Faure died in 1899 whilst in the throes of a sexual act with his mistress, Marguerite Steinheil, in the *salon bleu* in the private quarters of the presidential Palais de l'Élysée. The exact nature of the act is not known for sure, but, if rumours are to be believed, Steinheil was performing oral sex upon the President at the time of his death: the rigor he suffered caused his fingers to tangle in her hair, to the degree that assistance had to be called to remove them.

Alexander Douglas-Hamilton, 10th Duke of Hamilton, had a long interest in Ancient Egypt. He acquired a sarcophagus and asked that upon his death he be mummified. The Duke's wishes were complied with when he died in 1852, but the sarcophagus was found to be too small for him: his feet had to be broken at the ankles and folded inwards so that he could fit.

James Douglas, 4th Earl of Morton, introduced 'The Maiden', a predecessor of the guillotine, while he was regent of Scotland. Found guilty of complicity in the murder of the husband of Mary, Queen of Scots, in 1581, Douglas was executed on the very device he had introduced.

Recorded in the Proceedings of the Royal Society is the case of Mr John Davis of Birmingham, who, in 1862, fed a piece of tobacco, wrapped in bread, to an elephant. Davis laughed so much at the animal's displeasure that he fell dead from heart failure.

Allan Pinkerton, the founder of the world-famous Pinkerton National Detective Agency, died in 1884 after tripping over: the fall caused him to bite his tongue, and he died of the gangrene that set in as a result.

South African Victor Villenti was keen on health and healthy eating – indeed, he and his family were all vegetarians. While out jogging in 1991, he met a surprising fate: an 8lb leg of frozen lamb – which was being placed on a third-storey window ledge to defrost – dropped on Victor and killed him.

An American statesman (and one of the founders of the United States), Gouverneur Morris died in 1816 after pushing a piece of whale bone through his urinary tract to relieve a blockage.

Experienced skydiver Lester McGuire of Durham, North Carolina, was so preoccupied with the video equipment he was going to use during his latest skydive in 1988 that he apparently forgot to put on his parachute. He got wonderful pictures of his initial freefall; jerking motions then reveal his frantic attempts to reach around for the rip cord that was not there, and acceleration to the final impact with the ground at 150mph.

A London man died of a ruptured spleen in 1989 after a fatal encounter with a vegetable: his rib was shattered by a turnip, thrown out of a speeding car, which struck him whilst he was out walking near his home in Leytonstone.

Two women were sheltering under a tree during a thunder storm in Hyde Park in 1999 when, tragically, a lightning strike was drawn to the metal in their underwired bras. It killed them both instantly. Coroner Paul Knapman stated that, of over 50,000 deaths he had reviewed, it was only the second such occasion he had encountered such injuries.

In 2002 a Croatian man was killed when he took a chainsaw to a hand grenade – he was attempting to get the gunpowder out so that he could make some fireworks for New Year.

In 1923, Mrs Ruth Evans of Billington, Bedfordshire, was knocking a perambulator spring back in with a hammer when the spring caused the hammer to rebound: it struck her on the head, and she was killed by her own blow.

Elderly Andrew Berry of Wickford, Essex, changed an electric light bulb in his house in 1930. In doing so, he placed the old bulb on his armchair, promptly forgot about it – and sat down on it later that same day. The bulb shattered into Mr Berry's leg and cut him so badly that he died shortly afterwards in Southend Hospital.

Forty-one-year-old Maltese man Paul Gauci died in 1981 after welding a Second World War butterfly bomb to a metal pipe and using it as a mallet, thinking it was just a harmless can.

Multi-award-winning American author Tennessee Williams died in February 1983 when he choked on an eye-drop bottle-cap in his room at the Hotel Elysée in New York. Apparently, the author would routinely place the cap in his mouth and lean backwards before applying the drops. On this fatal night the cap fell down his throat.

In April 1985, twenty-two-year-old David Cooper was preparing to work on a 500,000-gallon slurry tank of liquefied cow manure on his family farm near Fombell, Pennsylvania. Unfortunately, however, David fell in. He drowned in the effluvia, his body only being retrieved after a rescue effort involving over 100 farmers and volunteer firemen.

Joseph LaRose was killed while delivering ice cream to a supermarket in Tampa, Florida, in 1991. The cause of his demise was a 500lb rack of 'Nutty Buddies' which toppled over onto him, breaking his leg and crushing his skull.

Kenneth 'Mr Hands' Pinyan, a resident of Gig Harbour of Seattle, Washington, died of acute peritonitis in 2005 after suffering a perforated colon while receiving anal intercourse from a stallion.

In 2008, a Manchester inquest concluded that a sixty-three-year-old resident of Ladybarn, Didsbury, had died as a result of picking his nose, causing it to bleed so severely that he bled to death.

A fifty-year-old Southampton man did not want to move out of his condemned block of flats in Bishopstoke. He held out here until the bitter end. In 2008, now the last resident in the building, he cut off his own head with a chainsaw to highlight what he saw as the injustice of forcing him to move out.

Wigan window cleaner Mark Fairhurst suffered a heart attack while working at the home of a customer in June 2006. Unfortunately she was out at the time: she returned to discover the window cleaner dead, with his head in his bucket. The inquest returned a verdict of accidental death.

Twenty-eight-year-old Jennifer Strange of Sacramento, California, was determined to win a Nintendo Wii console in a KDND 107.9 'The End' radio station's 'Hold Your Wee for a Wii' contest in 2007. The competition involved drinking large quantities of water without urinating, and poor Jennifer died of water intoxication during her attempt.

In August 2012, the *Telegraph* reported that 'a man who dressed up as Bigfoot to try to provoke reports of a sighting of the ape-like creature in Montana' had been run over as he stood in the road. A second car then ran over his body. The man, who had been wearing 'a military-style Ghillie suit consisting of strips of camouflage fabric' (used to camouflage snipers), was identified by Flathead County officials as Randy Lee Tenley, forty-four. Trooper Jim Schneider said that 'alcohol may have been a factor'. 'You can't make it up,' he continued. 'Obviously, his suit made it difficult for people to see him.'

THE STUFF OF NIGHTMARES

As surgical resident Dr Hitoshi Christopher Nikaidoh followed physician's assistant Karin Steinau into an elevator in the George W. Strake building at St Joseph Medical Centre in Houston, Texas, USA, in August 2003, the doors closed, pinning his shoulders fast. Nikaidoh appeared to struggle, attempting to shrug himself free from the grip of the doors (or possibly pull himself inside) but the elevator kept moving upward. What happened next was the stuff of nightmares: in seconds, his head hit the ceiling, and the majority of his head was sliced off. His left ear, lower lip, teeth and jaw were still attached to his body, which fell to the bottom of the elevator shaft. The elevator, containing the rest of the doctor, continued moving ever-upward as the horrified Steinau hammered at the panel of buttons. The accident was blamed on improper maintenance.

REVENGE

According to the Orkneyinga saga, Viking leader Sigurd the Mighty challenged a native ruler, Máel Brigte the Bucktoothed, to a forty-man-a-side battle in AD 892. Sigurd actually brought eighty men to the fight and put the opposition to a bloody end. Having defeated Máel Brigte, Sigurd beheaded him and strapped the head to his saddle as a trophy. However, Sigurd was not to have the last laugh for as he rode Máel Brigte's buck-tooth grazed his leg. The leg became infected, and as a result Sigurd died too.

THE FICKLE FINGER OF FATE

Thirty-seven-year-old cafeteria cook William Curry of Boston, Massachusetts, was overjoyed when he won $3.6 million in the state lottery in 1990. He decided not to give up his day job, though he did take a short holiday to celebrate the win. He then collected the first instalment of his winnings – and dropped dead on his first day back at work.

THE STUFF OF URBAN LEGEND

Twenty-one-year-old John Kemper Hutcherson of Marietta, Georgia, USA, drove off a road soon after leaving a bar at about midnight in August 2004. As he sped along, Hutcherson struck a kerb and hit the support wire to a telephone pole. The guide wire tore off the wing mirror and severed the head of his friend, Franky Brohm, who was sitting in the seat beside him. Hutcherson drove the 12 miles to his home and went inside to bed. At about 8.30 a.m. a neighbour walking his one-year-old daughter discovered the decapitated body in the truck and called the police. Brohm's head was recovered by the police later that same morning near the crash site. When police arrived at Hutcherson's house he claimed that he had not noticed the accident.

CACTUS CALAMITY

David M. Grundman went out into the desert in Phoenix, Arizona, in 1982 and used one of the giant saguaro cacti for target practice. Not the cleverest or the most legal thing to do – the cactus is a protected species – for, as he was firing off his last round, the massive upper section of the particular 26ft cactus he was blasting away at toppled over onto Grundman, causing him a very prickly death.

THE HASTE OF A PETULANT CHEF

François Vatel, the chef credited with the creation of Crème Chantilly, was very precious about his creations. In April 1671 he was charged with creating a banquet to honour King Louis XIV. On the evening in question there was a minor hitch with the preparations: a small seafood delivery arrived, but the rest was delayed. Under the misapprehension that the first delivery represented all the fish that was available, Vatel broke down. Dramatically exclaiming, 'I cannot endure this disgrace!' Vatel stomped off to his chamber, closed the door upon the handle of his sword and threw himself upon the point of the blade. His body was discovered by a cook who came to tell him that the rest of the fish had arrived.

SEA-SNAKE PORRIDGE

Gourmet Chef Le Hung Cuong plucked a venomous sea snake from a tank at a restaurant in Haiphong, Vietnam, in 2002, ready to turn it into that night's special: 'porridge with snake's blood'. The snake, however, had other plans: it lashed around and bit Cuong's left hand. He died on his way to hospital. Restaurant owner Nguyen Lien commented sympathetically: 'It was bad luck for him and for our restaurant; he was careless and did not put on the plastic gloves as required.'

STONEWALL

General Thomas J. 'Stonewall' Jackson, one of the most gifted tactical commanders of the American Civil War, was probably the best chance the Confederate states had to lead them to victory – but then came Major John D. Barry of the 18th North Carolina Infantry Regiment. Jackson and his staff were returning to camp under cover of darkness on the night of 2 May 1863 when they were challenged by a sentry. Jackson's staff gave the correct reply but before they knew what had hit them, Barry declared, 'It's a damned Yankee trick! Fire!' And fire they did. Jackson was badly wounded as a result. It is thought Stonewall was already suffering from pneumonia and had little chance of recovery. He died on 10 May.

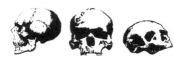

FATAL RSI?

At the inquest into the death of Mrs Elizabeth Alice Gregory, held at Stepney in 1934, Mr A.S. Weston, medical officer for the Mile End Hospital, stated that Mrs Gregory's work as a cleaner at the London Hospital, carried out over the previous ten years, had given her 'housemaid's knee'. This in turn had been the cause of her demise. Dr Guthrie, the coroner, queried this opinion: 'It is very rare to get a death from it, is it not?'

'Yes, very rare,' replied Weston.

The coroner thus recorded 'death by misadventure', adding that it was 'consequent upon her kneeling on the floor to do her work as a scrubber.'

FREAK OF NATURE?

Cleethorpes boiler-maker George Beeson was killed in 1923 as a result of what witnesses described as 'a ball of fire, probably three feet in diameter' that they saw 'rolling across the sky' until it struck a chimney stack: an explosion ensued, the stack shattered, the roof of the building tore open and the windows blew out. The unfortunate Mr Beeson was discovered amongst the debris, his skull fractured by a falling tile.

CRUSHED UNDER THE MISSUS

An inquest before the Liverpool City coroner in 1903 touched upon the deaths of William and Emily Shortis. The couple, who were in their late sixties, had been missed for a few days, and an entry was made into their home by a police officer. The couple were found at the bottom of the stairs. Emily was a large woman who had apparently died as she was going up the stairs; she had been followed up by her husband, and fell on to him. The dead weight of Mrs Shortis had injured her husband badly: the slightly-built man had been pinned under her on the stairs for three days. He died shortly after being discovered. Inquest returned a verdict of 'accidental death' for both.

THE CURSE OF CIGARETTES

Professional rodeo rider Wayne McLaren, who posed for photographs advertising Marlboro cigarettes in 1976, and the actor David McLean, who played the 'Marlboro Man' in the adverts for the cigarettes in the early 1960s, both died of lung cancer.

FLYING NOVELTY LAWNMOWER

Twenty-year-old John Bowen of Nashua, New Hampshire, went to watch a Jets-Patriots American football game at Shea Stadium in December 1979. The half-time show was a display of radio-controlled aircraft and novelties. The show had been staged on numerous occasions at a variety of venues, but on this occasion the operator of the flying lawnmower lost control: the model aircraft ploughed into the crowd, killing Bowen and seriously injuring another spectator.

A GOOD TURN

According to a report published in the *Sunday Observer* in 1925, an unfortunate accident claimed the life of French farmer M. Bousquet as he was overseeing work at a saw mill near Riberac. As some of his trees were being sawn into planks at the mill, he noticed a sow in the yard had become tangled in its chain and he stooped to free it. As the farmer attempted to do his good deed, the distressed animal butted him so violently his body was tossed a distance of 9ft, hurling him beneath the circular saw. His body was cut in two before the machinery could be stopped.

BITTEN TO DEATH

When innkeeper Herr Derer presented the bill for six quarts of beer to a customer at his pub in Elsbach, Western Bavaria, in 1936, the customer, Oskar Zaettel, did not react well. The men quarrelled: it came to blows, and Zaettel bit Derer hard on the neck. Infection rapidly set in, and Derer died. The courts were sympathetic, however, and Zaettel was given just three years of prison time.

LAMPED

Twenty-four-year-old Phillip Quinn of Kent, Washington, USA, was heating up his lava lamp upon the kitchen stove in 2004 when it exploded, sending deadly shards of glass into his body – one of which pieced his heart and killed him. Why he was heating the lamp in the first place remains a mystery.

SUPER-HOT CHILLI

Thirty-three-year-old Andrew Lee of Edlington, Doncaster, was a fork-lift driver by day and keen amateur chef by night. He went to his girlfriend's house in 2008 to cook up a chilli. Joined by her brother, Lee was challenged to eat a super-hot chilli for a bet; this he did, suffering heart failure the following morning.

KILLER KARAOKE

Father Robert del Rosario had just walked out from a refreshing dip in the sea at the resort of Morong in the Philippines in 2008 when he went to take part in a karaoke competition. When he took hold of the microphone to do so, however, it shorted out. Onlookers watched in horror as the current passed through him. Rosario collapsed and was declared dead on arrival at hospital.

HOLDING ON TOO LONG

The brilliant Danish astronomer and alchemist Tycho Brahe was attending a banquet in Prague in October 1601 when the call of nature struck. The problem was that to leave the banquet table would have been a terrible breach of etiquette. He therefore held his water all night but found, when he got home, that his water would no longer flow. Eventually he managed to squeeze out some, but only a small quantity, and not without excruciating pain. His kidneys soon went into decline and he died painfully over the next few days.

A DEADLY EMBRACE

In December 2008, Adelaide housewife Rajini Narayan was furious and vowed revenge after she saw her husband hug another woman. As he slept, she doused his genitals with petrol and set them alight. Husband Satish awoke in agony and leaped out of bed – knocking over the bottle of petrol and starting a fire that not only burnt his house down but caused him 85 per cent burns, injuries which proved fatal.

REPORTS OF MY DEATH...

Jamaican political leader Marcus Garvey Jr, it is claimed, perished in June 1940 after reading uncomplimentary and erroneous obituaries about him: the reports made him so angry that he suffered two strokes.

UPON HIS OWN PETARD

Pioneering American mechanical engineer, inventor and chemist Thomas Midgley Jr died in 1944 when he accidentally strangled himself with the ropes of a pulley-operated mechanical bed he had designed.

DENTURE DANGER

A sixty-five-year-old father of two from Brighton was choked to death by his own dentures whilst trying to chew a chicken kebab in 2008.

ROYAL DEATHS

According to Plutarch, Alexander the Great died in 323 BC as a result of a twenty-four-hour drinking binge with Medius of Larissa.

William the Conqueror was so bloated after his death in 1087 that his body would not fit in the tomb created to receive it at the Abbaye aux Hommes, Caen, France. Two of his soldiers tried to force him in by jumping up and down on him, but this simply broke the King's back, causing his stomach to explode and filling the church with an acrid stench.

King Henry I died in December 1135, while he was in Normandy, after eating 'a surfeit of lampreys' (an eel like fish) of which he was rather fond. His body was sewn into the hide of a bull to preserve him for his return journey to England, and he was buried at Reading Abbey.

According to Henry of Huntingdon, writing in the 1120s, Saxon King Edmund Ironside went to defecate in his necessary house in 1016 when an assassin, concealed in the pit below, stabbed the King up the anus twice with a sharp dagger. He made his escape, leaving the weapon fixed in the unfortunate King's bowels after the final blow.

A number of claims have been made for the cause of the death of King John in 1216, among them poisoned ale, poisoned plums or even a 'surfeit of peaches'.

Alexander III of Scotland was killed one dark night in 1286 when his horse lost its footing and fell over a steep rocky embankment.

According to a story recorded by Thomas de la Moore, King Edward II was assassinated at Berkeley Castle in Gloucestershire on 11 October 1327 by the unusual method of a red-hot poker being thrust up his anus.

James II of Scotland was a modern artillery enthusiast. During the siege of Roxburgh Castle in 1460 the King attempted to fire one cannon, known as 'the Lion', which he'd personally imported from Flanders. It exploded and killed him.

King George I died of a paralytic stroke caused by indigestion, brought on by the melons he had consumed when he was not fully recovered from seasickness.

According to his German *valet de chambre*, King George II was a loud and garrulous farter. One evening in October 1760, as the King went about his business on his close stool, the valet heard a roar 'louder than the usual royal wind'. To his horror, upon entering the room he found His Majesty on the floor, toppled from the royal commode. The King was lifted on to his bed but died a short while later.

King George IV died in 1830 from the effects of obesity on his heart and alcoholic cirrhosis of the liver. However, he was also suffering from dropsy, gout, gallstones, blindness and an overdose of laudanum. He was sixty-seven. *The Times* was less than sympathetic when it wrote about his death: 'There never was an individual less regretted by his fellow-creatures than this deceased King. What eye has wept for him? What heart has heaved one throb of unmercenary sorrow? ... If he ever had a friend – a devoted friend in any rank of life – we protest that the name of him or her never reached us.' How touching.

By 1737 Caroline, Queen Consort of George II, was a very unwell woman. Her demise was occasioned when one of her doctors bent too close to a lit candle and set his wig on fire: the Queen laughed so hysterically that her strangulated bowel burst and killed her.

The sporting Frederick, Prince of Wales, heir to the British throne, died from a burst abscess in the lung in 1751. The abscess has been commonly attributed to a blow by a cricket or a real tennis ball.

Adolf Frederick, King of Sweden, died of digestion problems on 12 February 1771 after having consumed a magnificent meal of lobster, caviar, sauerkraut, smoked herring and champagne, topped off with a massive fourteen servings of hetvägg, his favourite dessert, served in a bowl of hot milk. He is thus remembered by Swedish schoolchildren as 'the King who ate himself to death'.

King Alexandros I of Greece died from blood poisoning in 1920 after being bitten by two monkeys.

Two teenage Spanish princes, one Alfonso, the other later to become King Juan Carlos, went into a bedroom at the exiled royal family's home in Estoril, Portugal, with a loaded revolver in 1956. Juan Carlos was the only one to come out alive. What happened remains a mystery, though the official statement was this: 'While Prince Alfonso was cleaning a revolver with his brother, a shot went off which hit him in the forehead and killed him within a few minutes.'

King Haakon VII of Norway died in 1957 as a result of slipping on the soap in his bathroom.

As King George V lay on his deathbed in 1936 his personal physician, Lord Dawson, administered fatal doses of morphine and cocaine to assure him a painless death in time, according to Dawson's notes, for the announcement to be carried 'in the morning papers rather than the less appropriate evening journals.'

After the King's death, it was reported his last words had come in the form of a question to his private secretary: 'How is the Empire?' However, Dawson's notes report a subsequent exclamation, made whilst he was injecting His Majesty with a small dose of morphine to enable him to sleep more easily: 'God damn you,' said the King, as he fell asleep.

BRITISH PRIME MINISTERS
WHO DIED WHILE IN OFFICE

Spencer Compton, 1st Earl of Wilmington (1743)
Henry Pelham (1754)
Charles Watson-Wentworth, 2nd Marquess of Rockingham (1782)
William Pitt the Younger (1806)
Spencer Percival (assassinated in 1812)
George Canning (1827)
Henry Temple, 3rd Viscount Palmerston (1865)

LINCOLN AND KENNEDY ASSASSINATIONS

A list of as many as sixty coincidences between the assassinations of American Presidents Abraham Lincoln and John F. Kennedy started to appear in the mainstream American press from about a year after the assassination of JFK. Many of the claimed coincidences have now been debunked, but some still remain true, among them:

Abraham Lincoln and John F. Kennedy were elected to Congress a century apart – Lincoln in 1846 and Kennedy in 1946.

Abraham Lincoln and John F. Kennedy were elected President of the United States a century apart – Lincoln in 1860 and Kennedy in 1960.

Both wives of the Presidents lost a child while in the White House (Lincoln actually lost two children).

Both Presidents were shot on a Friday.

Both were shot in the head while seated.

Both were succeeded by Southerners.

Both successors were named Johnson – Andrew Johnson succeeded Lincoln, and Lyndon Johnson succeeded Kennedy.

Booth ran from the theatre and was caught in a warehouse, while Oswald ran from a warehouse and was caught in a movie theatre.

Both Booth and Oswald were killed before their trials.

TEN PRESIDENTS WHO DIED WHILE IN OFFICE

Zachary 'Old Rough and Ready' Taylor, President of the United States (1850)
Próspero Fernández Oreamuno, President of Costa Rica (1885)
Remigio Morales Bermúdez, President of Peru (1894)
Federico Errázuriz Echaurren, President of Chile (1901)
Gabriel Narutowicz, President of Poland (1922)
Ho Chi Minh, President of North Vietnam (1969)
Gamal Abdel Nasser, President of Egypt (1970)
Georges Pompidou, President of France (1974)
Omar Bongo Ondimba, President of Gabon (2009)
Bingu wa Mutharika, President of Malawi (2012)

WHERE'S HAROLD?

Prime Ministers don't just go missing… do they? Fifty-nine-year-old Australian Prime Minister Harold Holt went swimming off Cheviot Beach, near Portsea, Melbourne, Australia, on 17 December 1967. The sea was rough and friends warned Harold not to go into the water. He was never seen again, despite one of the largest search operations in Australian history. Holt was presumed dead; theories about what happened to him range from abduction by aliens to suicide, kidnap, and conspiracy by – or defection to – a foreign power. However, he was most likely eaten by a shark.

FAMOUS LAST WORDS

At a convivial night at the Three Turks at Charing Cross, Norwich, in October 1835, local artisan William Cork was singing the song composed upon the death of General Wolfe when, after repeating the words, 'And I to death must yield', he instantly fell down and died.

THE MORAL IS?

In 1928, Rouen mother Mme Blot despaired at her twenty-one-year-old daughter's desire to go to Paris and lead what she considered to be an immoral life. The girl told her that she was old enough to choose her own way of life, and that she would go no matter what her mother said. Failing to move her daughter's resolve, Mme Blot instead got a revolver and shot her dead. The mother was tried for the crime but was acquitted as it was considered to be 'an act carried out under extreme provocation'.

BELL ENDS

In December 1728 Henry West, the bell ringer of King's College, Cambridge, was crushed to death by one of the five great bells of the college. In a similar but unrelated incident in February 1806, James Coleman was tolling the bell in the parish church at Swardeston in Norfolk when the crown and cannons broke from the bell, sending it crashing through the floor and killing him on the spot.

FLAT LINING

By some terrible accident, eighteen-year-old George Crane died when his head was crushed by a steam roller on Norwich Road, Ipswich, in April 1907.

THE HUMAN OSTRICH

Robert Naysmith was a sideshow performer who, under the *nom de plume* 'the Human Ostrich', amazed crowds by swallowing nails, hatpins, hairpins, stones and even shards of glass. After years of this terrible diet he became ill and could no longer perform his act, so he took to selling bootlaces. When Naysmith died – of gastritis and peritonitis – in Islington Workhouse in 1906, a post-mortem revealed that he still had more than thirty nails and hatpins in his body. Some of them were in his liver and kidneys, but the majority were lodged in his intestines.

DEATH AT THE BANK OF ENGLAND

An inquest was held at the Bank of England before the City of London coroner into the death of Charles Rose, comptroller of the

Stock Department, in 1887. Evidence revealed that, after eating a large breakfast, Mr Rose had had to run to catch his train. When he arrived he complained of stomach pains and vomited. Medicine was procured from a neighbouring chemist's shop; Rose drank it and said he felt better, but he was subsequently found lying dead on the floor of his room. The surgeon who had conducted the post-mortem pronounced, 'Death was due to a syncope brought on by the deceased eating a hearty meal and then hurrying to catch his train.'

BACON AND THE FOWL

Lord Francis Bacon, natural philosopher, statesman and scientist, was pondering his latest research into the conservation and induration of bodies during his ride between Holborn and Highgate in London one snowy morning in March 1626. Seized by the idea of conducting an experiment to see if cold could preserve flesh from putrefaction, he purchased a fowl and proceeded to stuff its crop with snow. The results of this experiment may have proved valuable for mankind but poor Lord Bacon caught a chill in the process; the sickness progressed apace, and he died on 9 April 1626.

SYNCHRONICITY?

Recorded on a headstone in Whitby, North Yorkshire, is the following inscription:

Here lie the bodies of Francis Huntrodds and Mary his wife, who were both born on the same day of the week, month and year (viz.) Sepr ye 19th 1600, marry'd on the day of their birth and after having had 12 children born to them died aged 80 years on the same day of the year they were born, September ye 19th 1680, the one not one above five hours before ye other.

MASTER CRAFTSMAN

John Willson, the man responsible for the erection of a 15ft-tall Coade-stone statue of George III atop the old land lighthouse column at Dunston, Lincolnshire stood back to admire his completed work on 9 September 1810 – and fell to his death down the 90ft of the rest of the column.

OUT OF THE CLOSET

The locked door of a lumber room in Caius College, Cambridge, was finally opened on 9 November 1789. The problem had been that the Revd Samuel Reeve MA, Fellow and Senior Proctor of the University, was the only person to have a key and he had not been seen since 1 July. He was found inside, hanging by the neck.

THE MAD BUTCHER

A dreadful event occurred whilst a butcher named Henry Briggs was awaiting removal to a lunatic asylum at Ely Workhouse, Cambridgeshire, in January 1876. Seizing a red-hot poker from the fire Briggs thrust it several times into his body. He then rushed at the attendants, who fled. One of them dropped a pocket knife as he ran – with which the distracted man cut his throat from ear to ear. He died of his injuries the following day.

THE FATAL COAL SCUTTLE

The Lincoln coroner held an inquest upon the body of John Edward Hill in 1899. Hill had been bathing in the river with some friends, in quite shallow water, when he ducked under the surface. Tragically, however, in doing so he caught his body against an old coal scuttle at the bottom of the water and tore open his abdomen to such an extent that his bowels protruded. He was removed to hospital, where another wound was found in his large intestine and all hopes of his recovery were abandoned. The poor fellow lingered for three days before he finally expired.

A CURIOUS SUICIDE

Bury St Edmunds shopkeeper Robert Wham decided to take his own life in February 1872. He was found with a leather strap wound twice around his neck and attached to a beam in the shop. His feet were touching the ground, despite his knees being bent. In fact, it appeared he had been apprehensive as to whether his body weight would be sufficient to cause his death, and so he'd attached a 4lb weight about his body. Prior to suspending himself, he had also run a piece of wire, taken from a ginger-beer bottle, through his nose and fastened it to a hook that was hanging from a nail in the beam. The inquest into his death concluded 'suicide while in a state of insanity'.

THE FLYING PERFORMER

On 26 May 1863 vocalists Charles Marsh and Henry Wharton attempted to ascend the Nelson Monument at Great Yarmouth, Marsh performing 'God Save the Queen' on his violin as he went, with Wharton accompanying on his banjo. Both arrived at the summit but Marsh went on to scale the figure of Britannia. Achieving this feat, he stood atop the figure, waving to the crowd beneath, but in descending he lost his grasp of Britannia's trident handle – he slipped, fell from the plinth, rebounded into space and fell with his arm outstretched to the base of the column, some 114ft below. His death was recorded as 'instantaneous'.

MISS BASSETT THE PARACHUTIST

Miss Adelaide 'Addie' Bassett (thirty-six), a London parachutist, was killed at a fête and gala held at Peterborough in August 1895. The display, which consisted of a balloon ascent and a double parachute descent, was billed as 'A Race for Life' and was to be performed by Captain Alfred Orton and Miss Bassett. As the balloon ascended it was noticed that a telephone wire had caught on Miss Bassett's parachute, causing it to turn upside down. At a height of 60ft they jumped. Captain Orton's parachute allowed him to glide to earth but because they were jumping from such a low height the crucial seconds lost by the inversion of her parachute meant Miss Bassett's did not inflate correctly. She fell, head-first, hitting the ground with a sickening thud. Her corpse was removed to the nearest infirmary. This terrible scene was witnessed by thousands of spectators.

ON THE RAILS

John Jubb, a platelayer who had been employed for many years on the Great Central Railway, was walking over the Trent Railway Bridge at Bole on 2 January 1900 for the purpose of fog signalling. Hearing a train coming he stepped across to the other set of rails – where he was instantly knocked down and killed by the 11.37 Great Eastern Express from Doncaster. Unfortunately there were two trains coming at the same time: the fog had been so dense that neither engine driver could see any distance ahead. Poor John Jubb didn't have a hope.

IN MEMORY OF

OUR COMRADES

KILLED AT 'FOGG'S PIT,'
OCTOBER 4TH, 1907. . .

MY dear comrades one and all
I appeal to you though great or small,
I'm doing this for charity's sake,
For one never knows, it might be our fate.

At ' Fogg's Colliery' (Oct. 4th),
There was a sad accident which we all know :
Ten poor Colliers who had finished for the day
Were returning to the surface to receive their
scanty pay.

Little did they know When they got in the
cage to ride,
They would never reach the top,
Not one of them alive

It looks very hard, 'tis sad to relate,
After working all day,
They deserved a better fate.

There is no one knows the risks,
Like those who work in the mine,
But we must all go some day,
When it comes our time.

But somebody must get the coal,
No matter who it be ;
For you can just lose your life the same,
Whatever your occupation might be.

So let us hope that all the people,
In this little Colliery Town,
Will think about those little ones at home.
For it makes a home feel sad,
When they have parted with their dad,
We should think so if it was our own

38 Bow Street,   Written and Composed by
Bolton.   MR. JOHN CARROLL.

UNFORTUNATE TIMING

In May 1876 Samuel Watson was a young and sober porter removing the tail lamp from a train at the GER Station at Bury St Edmunds in Suffolk. As he was moving away, the train backed up and Watson was fatally crushed between the buffers.

GETTING INTO A PICKLE

In February 1832 Thomas Foyson was working at his small family vinegar works on Calvert Street, Norwich, when he was overcome by the fumes from the vat of vinegar he was gauging and he fell in. By the time he was extracted he was not only dead from drowning but well pickled too.

IMPRISONED IN ICE

On 2 February 1799, Elizabeth Woodcock of Impington managed to wade her way through deep snow to Cambridge Saturday Market, where she sold her eggs and butter. After replenishing her flask with brandy at the Three Tuns on Castle Hill, she set off home. Just outside Impington she was thrown from her horse and, being shaken by the fall and numbed by the freezing cold, she was unable to remount. She took shelter under a hedge, but the snow began to drift and soon she was completely entombed. As hours and days passed, she heard the church bells and the voices of people in the distance. On the Monday she summoned enough energy to tie her red handkerchief to a stick and push it up through a gap in the snow. This makeshift flag did lead to her discovery – but not for another week! William Munsey, the parish clerk of Impington, spotted the 'flag', discovered the frozen Elizabeth and summoned help. Mrs Woodcock had spent eight days buried in the snow and lived to tell the tale – but not for long. She was taken ill and died on 24 July, aged forty-three.

THE BOTTESFORD PRIVY TRAGEDY

The floor of the privy of the Bull Inn at Bottesford, Lincolnshire, was made of wood placed over a vault that was some 3 or 4yds in depth. Fatefully, even though it had been in an insecure state for some time, nothing had been done to preserve it. During the afternoon of 30 April 1831 four children, aged between nine and twelve years of age, went into the privy. They were dancing upon the floor when, suddenly, it gave way, taking the children down with it: all were suffocated in the soil and effluvia before help could be obtained.

MR CLEAN

One reclusive resident of Didsbury, Manchester, had become obsessed with using the well-known cleaning product and disinfectant Dettol. He had hundreds of bottles of the stuff in his flat, and used copious amounts of it to clean his home – the place reeked of it. He even used Dettol to wash himself, regularly, every day. Such over-exposure to the cleaning agent resulted in too little oxygen getting into his system, which proved fatal in 2007. So powerful was the pong of disinfectant when his body was discovered that a number of the police officers who went into the flat following his death later took sick leave, suffering with aches and pains after being 'overpowered' by the smell.

DOES THIS GUN WORK?

A report published in the *Ipswich Journal* in 1805 told of an inquest held on the body of John Nutter. He had been visiting William Lister's shop to purchase a clock for a friend when he spotted a gun and picked it up to examine it. Nutter declared that the lock of the gun was of a poor quality, but Mr Lister contended it was a good one and never misfired. To demonstrate this, Lister cocked the weapon and pulled the trigger – but forgot that it was fully charged with powder and shot. The discharge of the weapon struck Nutter in the lower part of the belly. He died the following day. It must have been some small consolation to him to know that the gun did work reliably after all.

SPIDER IN THE CHIMNEY

The Bear Hotel in Stock, Essex, is a fine old English inn. Its greatest character lived in the nineteenth century: an ostler named Charlie Marshall, known to his friends as 'Spider'. If you stood him an evening's drinks, or offered a wager, he would crawl up the chimney in one bar and come down the chimney in the other. If he was feeling particularly coy he would stay up there until a fire was lit to drive him down again. One Christmas Day, perhaps after too much feasting, he attempted his usual feat. His audience waited and waited; they even lit fires, but he never came down again. His well-cured remains are said to be somewhere in the pub's chimneys to this day.

ACT OF GOD

Little Mary Haselton, aged nine, was a child of devout Catholic parents and had been brought up to loyally observe her devotions. On 16 August 1785 Mary was in the act of prayer, repeating her Vespers, when there was a flash of lightning and she was killed instantly. Her memorial tablet, which relates this tragic tale, may still be seen on the wall of the Charnel House in the graveyard in Bury St Edmunds, Suffolk.

A RINGER'S DOOM

Mary Hill died while ringing one of the four bells at Springthorpe church, Lincolnshire, on Shrove Tuesday in 1814. By some accident she had been drawn up to the roof and fell to the floor, hitting a large stone that now forms the base of the font. Three 'Maidens' Crowns', three garlands and three white gloves were carried at her funeral by three maidens dressed in white. These symbols were carried as a mark of her chastity.

THUNDERSTRUCK

A farmer's son and five labourers were ploughing in a field at Barrington in Cambridgeshire in May 1867 when a thunderstorm rolled over them. As they were taking shelter under a nearby straw stack one flash of lightning rendered them all insensible. All revived except a Mr Patman, who had caught the majority of the lightning strike and was found to be lifeless, 'his shoes, leggings and hat torn to atoms.' In another incident in the same county in 1873, William Ison was struck by lightning and killed while cutting hay upon Quy Fen; a stone, which may still be seen, was erected on the spot to commemorate that tragic event.

MORE LIGHTNING

An epitaph on a gravestone at Stanton Harcourt, Oxfordshire states:

> Near this place lie the bodies
> Of John Hewit and Sarah Drew
> An industrious young man and virtuous young maiden of this parish;
> Who being at harvest work [with several others]
> Were in one instant killed by lightning.
> The last day of July, 1718.

TWO SERGEANTS STANDING IN THE SUN

Egyptian Campaign soldier Sergeant Allen of 1st Battalion, the Coldstream Guards, while at Pirbright, and Sergeant Kendall of 4th Volunteer Battalion, the East Surrey Regiment, near Bisley Common, were both seized by sun stroke and died as a result in June 1895.

PRANKED TOO FAR

Thai garage worker Charnchai Puanmuangpak died when two of his co-workers thought it would be funny to insert the nozzle of a compressed air pump up his rectum while he was in a deep sleep during a break in 1993. The ensuing intense blast of air punctured his intestine. He was dead before he reached the hospital.

HAPPY NEW YEAR

William Rhodes (twenty-four), mate of the sloop *Queen of Louth and Grimsby*, had been drinking at the house of the father of a young woman to whom he was about to be married on New Year's Eve 1852. When he returned to his vessel in the river at Louth in Lincolnshire, Rhodes was the worse for drink. He went to the bows to defecate, strained too hard, fell overboard and drowned.

2

MYSTERIOUS DEATHS

STABBED – BUT HOW?

A blind Cambridgeshire pensioner, named Lavinia Farrar and said to be 'of independent means', was found on her kitchen floor with her face bruised and nose broken in 1901. A blood-stained knife was found near the body and there were drops of blood on the floor. At the inquest two doctors testified that the woman had been stabbed in the heart – but there was no puncture in any of the four garments she was wearing over the wound. The stab to the heart would have caused almost instantaneous death, so there is no possibility that she might have stabbed herself and then got dressed before she perished. Nor could a knife have been inserted through the openings in her garments: their fastenings were too far apart. The blood on the knife and drops of blood on the floor were not from the woman's wound, as her wound was almost bloodless – only her innermost garment was very slightly blood-stained. There appeared to have been no robbery or motive for an attack. The jury returned an open verdict.

BODY IN A BARREL

In June 1880 a body was discovered crammed into an American barrel and covered in chloride of lime (no doubt in the mistaken belief this chemical would hasten decomposition) in the cellar of No. 139 Harley Street, London, the home of Jacob Quixona Henriques. Mr Henriques – who had lived at his Harley Street address for over twenty years – was astonished by the discovery and, despite evidence presented by the three butlers he had engaged over the years, no further light could be shed on how the barrel got there, how long it had been there or its occupant. The body discovered was that of a woman of forty years old. She was almost naked except for the remains of stockings and garters on her legs; the hair appeared to have been cut off. Dr Pepper of St Mary's Hospital stated that the cause of death was a stab wound in the chest made by 'such as a table knife.' A verdict of murder by person, or persons, unknown was recorded.

THE LEA MYSTERY

Elizabeth Ann Smith (twenty-five) was seen walking with a man described as 'a young toff' in Greyhound Gardens by the River Lea in London, during late April 1888. She was later seen that same evening dancing with the man at the nearby Carmen's Rest Coffee House, where she was remembered because she had passed out; she had to be revived with snuff. She was last spotted leaving a nearby pub and walking up the road in an apparent state of intoxication. She was accompanied by two men. Her body was found drowned in the river a week later. Despite one side of her face and a portion of her hand being consumed by rats, she was positively identified by her father. The men who had been seen with her were traced and put on trial for her murder but there was no clear evidence of foul play. Both were acquitted and the death of Miss Smith was recorded as a tragic accident.

UNDER THEIR NOSES

In October 1888 workmen discovered a human torso in one of the cellars of the New Scotland Yard building on the Embankment. Upon examination the trunk was found to be that of an adult female with her arms, legs and head cut off. Only the arms, minus the hands, were later recovered from the Thames. The rest of the body parts were never found. The torso was never identified and the perpetrator of this dastardly deed was never caught – thus the capital's new police headquarters was literally built on an unsolved mystery!

DEATH OF A POLICEMAN

Police Sergeant John Harvey was making routine enquiries in the Ardleigh area of Essex in January 1894. After walking a short distance with one of his constables, Sergeant Harvey was last seen at about 7.30 p.m. – he was never seen alive again. The following morning he was discovered down a snow-covered well in the garden of one of the cottages. His watch had stopped at 8.21 p.m. He had suffered injuries to his face but exactly how they were caused was never proved with any certainty and the death of Sergeant Harvey remains a mystery.

TIED UP

In February 1931 the dead body of first-year student Frederick John Charles Ellis was discovered in his room at Sidney Sussex College, Cambridge, lying fully clothed on the floor. His hands were found tied together behind his back with handkerchiefs and khaki puttees and his arms secured by electric flex. Further handkerchiefs were tied over his mouth and nostrils, all of them knotted in a methodical and neat fashion. His head was pushed into a thick cushion. Police enquires revealed Ellis had been involved in a 'craze' which had lasted for a couple of terms involving study experiments and competitions in binding one another with ropes and handkerchiefs to see who was the first to free themselves. At the inquest, pathologist Sir Bernard Spilsbury testified that, in his opinion, 'nobody else was responsible for the tying up' and 'there was no indication of anyone else having been in the room.' The jury retired for an hour and returned 'death by asphyxia due to an accident.'

PREMONITION OR CURSE?

When Granny Corbyn died at Fressingfield in Suffolk in April 1890 she proclaimed that her step-grandchild would not long survive her. The child's parents, Mr and Mrs Hammond, took the baby out for a walk a few hours after Granny's passing – and suddenly they were horrified to see foul-smelling smoke 'not unlike brimstone' issuing from the pram. The baby died, but all the inquest could conclude was that death had been caused by 'shock caused by some powerful irritant', though what this was, why and by whom it was applied was never determined. However, at the inquest elderly George Corbyn was to comment, 'I always believed my wife to be a witch.'

DID SHE FALL OR WAS SHE...?

The mysterious death of Mary Dickinson (eighty-six) at Bracebridge near Lincoln in February 1850 remains a mystery. The inquest, before Mr Hitchins, revealed Mrs Dickinson lived with her granddaughter Elizabeth Hoe and her husband, and that the elderly lady died from three incised wounds, one extending from under the throat, up the right cheek to the temple, and the others being similar cuts on the right arm. Mrs Hoe claimed that the cuts had been caused during a fall down the narrow stairs of the house into the kitchen. However, the Hoe's child denied that this fall had occurred. Mr Hill, the surgeon, deposed that the wounds had been the cause of death, but that they could not have been caused by a fall...

THE APPLE TREE

An inquest was held at Ely in 1839 upon the body of Martha Day, a girl of about thirteen. She had called to her mother the previous afternoon, at about 1 p.m; rushing outside, the mother found her daughter on a low branch of an apple tree in the orchard. On lifting her down from the tree, the horrified mother discovered that the girl could no longer stand and appeared to have lost the use of her limbs; before she could be carried into the house, she expired. The post-mortem revealed a dislocation at the first vertebra of the neck had occurred, causing total paralysis and almost instant death. The verdict was given accordingly.

END OF THE LAST WITCHMASTER

Old George Pickingill, the last Witchmaster of Canewdon in Essex, met his end in 1909 when he was said to be as old as 105. Pickingill went out walking on a dull and windy day. As he was strolling by the churchyard wall, his hat was blown over among the gravestones. According to the legend, as he was retrieving it the sun broke momentarily through the clouds and cast the shadow of a headstone in the shape of a cross over George's face. It killed him instantly.

THE GRANTHAM RAILWAY DISASTER

On 19 September 1906 a Great Northern Railway evening sleeping car and mail train was travelling on the East Coast mainline from London Kings Cross to Edinburgh's Waverley Station, hauled by Ivatt 'Atlantic' No. 276, when it derailed near Grantham, causing fourteen deaths and seventeen injuries.

The accident occurred in mysterious circumstances; the train had run right through Grantham Station, where it was scheduled to stop, and derailed on a sharp curve at the end of the platform. At the inquest it was agreed that both the driver and fireman were competent men to work the train but the evidence could not prove that the brakes had been applied in sufficient time to bring about a stop at Grantham.

A number of explanations for the cause of the accident have been suggested over the years: the driver going mad; being drunk; falling asleep; being taken ill; or having a fight with the fireman. However, the clear evidence given at the inquest by signalman Alfred Day at the south box, a quarter of a mile from Grantham Station, was that although the train appeared 'to be running too fast to stop at the station', he had seen both men looking through the cab's front windows, apparently calmly and in their normal positions. This opinion was echoed by Richard Scoffin (who had been in the employ of the GNR since 1890) who was in the north cabin, 129yds from the north end of Grantham Station platform. At the inquest both Frederick William Fleetwood, forty-five, the driver of the train, and Ralph Talbot, twenty-three, the fireman, received unreserved reports of good character, competency and reliability from Mr Martin Cole, the District Locomotive Superintendent at Doncaster, who had known both men for a number of years. No definite cause of the accident was ever established; indeed, it has been described by some railway historians as 'the railway equivalent of the *Marie Celeste*'.

SPONTANEOUS HUMAN COMBUSTION?

According to a report published in *The Gentleman's Magazine* in 1731, the sixty-two-year-old Countess Cornelia Bandi of Cesena was discovered dead in her bedchamber in Verona. The report states: 'The floor of the chamber was thick-smear'd with a gluish moisture, not easily got off... and from the lower part of the window trickl'd down a greasy, loathsome, yellowish liquor with an unusual stink.' But what of the poor Countess? Specks of soot hung in the air. Her bed was undamaged; the sheets were turned down, as if she had got out of bed, but nearby was 'a heap of ashes, two legs untouch'd, stockings on, between which lay the head, the brains, half of the back-part of the skull and the whole chin burn'd to ashes, among which were found three fingers blacken'd. All the rest was ashes which had this quality, they left in the hand a greasy and stinking moisture.'

In 1744 Grace Pett, a suspected witch of Ipswich in Suffolk, was believed to have laid a curse over a local farmer's sheep. Superstition held that redress against the witch could only be obtained by fastening one of the unfortunate animals to the ground, burying its feet in the earth, and then burning the rest of the beast. This done, the following morning Grace Pett's body was found lying on the floor near her hearth. She had been burned to cinders, with the exception of her hands and feet! Curiously, the boarded floor upon which she was found was not even scorched.

Elizabeth Smith of Brampton, Lincolnshire, was a habitual smoker and laudanum drinker who was prone to fits. In September 1889 her neighbours noticed smoke issuing from the house. They opened the door and found her body in bed, burnt to a cinder. Officially it was thought that Mrs Smith had been smoking in bed when she was seized by a fit: her pipe, it was thought, had fallen from her mouth and set her clothes alight. Curiously, little regard was paid to the fact that the bedclothes, save those in the immediate area of the fire, were undamaged.

In August 1938, Phyllis Newcombe, twenty-two, was attending a dance in Chelmsford, Essex. As she was leaving the floor, her dress suddenly flared up – and within seconds she was a blazing mass of blue flames. Her fiancé attempted to beat the flames out with his bare hands, but Phyllis was fatally burnt before the ambulance arrived.

Gas-meter-reader Don Gosnell was in December 1966 on his rounds in Coudersport, Pennsylvania, when he entered a house and went down to the basement of Dr John Irving Bentley. When Gosnell reached the basement his attention was drawn by some wisps of a light bluish smoke, a strange, sickly-sweet smell and a small hole in the upper floor through which had fallen a pile of ash. Going back up to investigate, Gosnell then discovered the charred remains of Dr Bentley in the bathroom: there was not much left of him bar cinders – only his lower right leg remained, with his slipper left on it. The rest of the room, bar the small hole in the floor, was untouched by the fire. His death was explained away as a visitation by lightning.

3

BODY-SNATCHERS

Unclaimed bodies from rivers, executed felons and suicides were all fair game for the dissectionist's table but such legitimate supplies by no means met the demands of the medical schools, and thus a dark business by dead of night soon emerged – body-snatching.

Body-snatchers, otherwise known as 'resurrectionists' or 'resurrection men', operated across most of Great Britain and were well paid for their trouble by medical schools or their surgical masters. Sir Astley Cooper (later appointed Professor of Anatomy to the Royal College of Surgeons, made personal physician to the monarch and a baronet) took quite some grim satisfaction in telling a House of Commons' investigation there was 'no person, whatever his situation might be, whose body, after death, I cannot obtain.'

THE BODY-SNATCHING RIOT

In April 1732 a grave was found robbed in Ditton churchyard, Cambridgeshire. It was rumoured the body had been delivered to Emmanuel College. Obtaining a warrant, a large number of Ditton folk marched on the college, but the mob was refused entry. The mob then attacked the walls; the students rose up to defend their territory, and violence erupted. The situation was so severe that the town clerk read the Riot Act; only then would the mob disperse. Later, Justice of the Peace Mr Pern granted a warrant for constables to search the entire college. No body was discovered, but the following morning the unfortunate corpse was found floating in the pond of the college close.

THE FIRST LONDON BODY-SNATCHERS

John Holmes, gravedigger at St George the Martyr, Queen Street, Bloomsbury, and his assistant, Robert Williams, were caught stealing the corpse of Mrs Jane Salisbury for dissection in October 1777. This became the first case of a London body-snatcher being brought to court. Both men were given sentences of six months and were ordered to be publicly whipped from Kingsgate Street to Dyott Street, St Giles.

YOU CAN'T BE TOO CAREFUL

The fear of being taken by body-snatchers was so great that some people went to extremes to keep their remains in the ground. In one instance, at King's Lynn, Norfolk, in February 1829, an individual was consigned to his grave with thirteen iron hoops around his coffin and the lid firmly closed with fifty screws.

A TALE OF PROVINCIAL BODY-SNATCHERS

In late December 1827, resurrectionist activities were detected in Great Yarmouth, Norfolk. George Beck, a local baker, was concerned to find his recently buried wife's grave apparently disturbed. Further investigation confirmed his worst fears – the body had been stolen by the resurrection men. Upon investigation, it was determined that about twenty graves had been tampered with. The body-snatching gang may have received warning of the discovery of their nocturnal activities and slipped away into the darkness but their leader, Thomas Vaughan, had 'behaved ill to a young woman to whom he passed himself off as a bachelor' and was detained. The rest of the gang were soon identified, as was their base, a rented house near St Nicholas' church and its graveyard. Among the other gang members were father and son team William and Robert Barber. The son, Robert, turned King's Evidence in a plea for leniency and told how he and his father robbed the graves, packed bodies in boxes and sent them, by wain (a type of cart), to London and named famous surgeon Sir Astley Paston Cooper as the final recipient of the corpses. The most adept member of the gang was a tall, strong Irishman named Murphy, who carried the bodies. He had been paid £12 12*s* each for at least four of the bodies from Yarmouth.

Astley Cooper and his fellow London surgeons did not forsake their resurrection men. A legal representative was sent to act on behalf of Vaughan for the grand sum, in those days, of £14. Vaughan was even sent 10*s* a week for the twenty-six weeks he was in confinement. Murphy was also well treated, and for his defence, at trial, the not-inconsiderable amount of £160 was also paid by the surgeons. Luckily for Vaughan, the relatively new crime of body-snatching had no specific legislature against it: to remove a body from a grave was not strictly illegal and could only be treated as a misdemeanour, for which crime he was found guilty. The maximum sentence of six months' imprisonment in the House of Correction was meted out. To apply a more robust approach to body-snatchers the law soon found a loophole: theft of property, i.e. the shroud in which the corpse had been wrapped. This, if bought and paid for, amounted to handling stolen property. An intriguing footnote is to be found in the ultimate fate of Vaughan: after his release he went to Plymouth, but he had not learned his lesson and fell foul of the law by '[there] appropriating the clothes in which a dead body had been wrapped'. Prosecuted for felony, he was transported to Australia.

BURKE AND HARE

The most notorious 'body-snatchers' of all were William Burke and William Hare, who sold their bodies to Dr Robert Knox, a private anatomy lecturer whose students were drawn from the Edinburgh Medical College. In fact, they did not dig up the bodies they sold. Their first body came when a tenant died owing rent at the lodging house kept by Hare's wife at Tanner's Close in the West Port area of Edinburgh. To recoup their losses, they sold his body to Knox. Discovering this was easy money, Burke and Hare set about 'easing' the sick, shuffling them off this mortal coil with

the aid of a suffocating pressure upon their chests. They then took the fresh bodies to the surgeon. Twelve months later the pair had built up quite a trade, but they were detected in their dark business and brought to trial. Hare (pictured opposite) was offered immunity from prosecution if he confessed and testified against Burke (above). This he did, saving his own neck but sending Burke to the gallows.

Burke was executed on 28 January 1829. Somewhat ironically, after execution his body was publicly dissected at the Medical College; his skeleton is still on display at the University of Edinburgh's Anatomical Museum. The term 'Burking' soon entered common parlance as another name for body-snatching.

KINGS OF BODY-SNATCHING:
THE LONDON BURKERS

John Bishop, Thomas Williams and James 'Blaze-Eye Jack' May were the infamous 'London Burkers'; they operated out of No. 3 Nova Scotia Gardens, Bethnal Green, in the early 1830s. Their method was similar to Burke and Hare, in that they turned to obtaining their bodies by murdering transient Londoners instead of robbing graves. Plying them with drink laced with laudanum, they took their unfortunate victims to Nova Scotia Gardens and drowned them in a static water tank buried in the back garden. They were caught after Blaze-Eye Jack got drunk and argued about the price of a body at the door of the dissecting rooms at King's College, Somerset House. Suspicious of the posture of the body, which looked more like that of a murder victim than a peacefully deceased person, the doctors sent for the Bow Street Runners. Tried at the Old Bailey in December 1831, Bishop and Head exonerated May from the act of killing and he was sentenced to the prison hulks, while Bishop and Williams were sent to the gallows. Before he kept his appointment with the hangman, Bishop confessed that he had trafficked nearly 1,000 bodies during his twelve-year career as a body-snatcher. Bishop and Williams also ended up on the dissecting tables they had supplied for so long.

THE BODY OF LAURENCE STERNE

The bodies dissected at the Cambridge anatomy amphitheatre on Queens' Lane were often obtained from body-snatchers who operated in other parts of the country. In March 1768 a body on the table caused a stir – the lecturer and a number of the students recognised it as the corpse of famous author Laurence Sterne, the author of *The Life and Opinions of Tristram Shandy, Gentleman*, who had died of consumption and had been buried in the new burial ground of St George's, Hanover Square, London, only a couple of days previously. The anatomisation was carried out nonetheless, but it appears the lecturer's conscience was troubled about the fate of the body of the author so he had it sent back to London for a discreet reburial. When the churchyard of St George's was redeveloped in the 1960s, Sterne's skull was disinterred, in a manner befitting the man who enjoyed the nickname 'Yorick', and was identified by the fact that it was the only skull, of the five in Sterne's grave, that bore evidence of having been anatomised. It was transferred to its final resting place in Coxwold churchyard, North Yorkshire, in 1969.

CHARLIE CHAPLIN

Body-snatching is not a crime of the past: sporadic instances still occur, such as the theft of the body of the great silent film star Charlie Chaplin from his grave in Vevey, Switzerland, in March 1978. The remains were held for a 600,000-franc ransom, which was demanded from his widow. She refused to pay. After a large police operation, the body-snatchers were traced and arrested, and Chaplin's remains were recovered from a cornfield in the nearby village of Noville. Chaplin was replaced in his grave – with 6ft of concrete poured on top for good measure.

4

AT THE HANDS
OF THE PHYSICIAN

Neglected by his doctor,
Ill-treated by his nurse,
His brother robbed the widow,
Which made it all the worse.
                    (Epitaph upon a gravestone in Dulverton, Somerset)

BACK AGAIN

Margaret Carpenter, a livery lace maker of Little Queen Street, Lincoln's Inn Fields, London, was pronounced dead and laid out in February 1767. That same night, movement was heard in the room where her body lay. Eerie footsteps were heard to cross the floor and descend the stairs, and her family trembled as the door of their room slowly began to open – to reveal the sadly-departed Margaret standing before them, naked and quite alive! When placed in a warmed bed she revived, but she continued to complain she was 'bitter cold'. The whole affair tragically proved too much for her, and she was dead – really dead, that is – a few days later.

THE HECKINGTON HYPOCHONDRIAC

Samuel Jessup, sixty-five, an opulent grazier of Heckington in Cambridgeshire, died on 17 May 1817. According to the evidence given upon a trial for the amount of an apothecary's bill, at the Lincoln Assizes, a short time before Mr Jessup's death, an astonishing statistic was revealed: over the past twenty-one years, between 1791 and 1816, Jessup had taken 226,934 pills. These had all been supplied by an apothecary at Bottesford in Lincolnshire. That equates with a rate of 10,806 pills a year, or 29 pills each day. However, it seems that Mr Jessup began with only a moderate appetite, one which increased as he proceeded, for in the five years preceding 1816 he took the pills at the rate of 78 a day; and in the year 1814, he swallowed not fewer than 51,590.

Notwithstanding this, and with the addition of 40,000 bottles of mixture, as well as 'julaps and electuaries', extending altogether to fifty-five closely written columns of an apothecary's bill, Mr Jessup lived to the age of sixty-five.

BLACK PLAGUE

The Black Death (bubonic plague) was one of the deadliest pandemics in human history and is estimated to have killed around half the population of Europe between 1348 and 1350. It was characterised by the appearance of buboes in the groin, neck and armpits – which all oozed pus and blood – accompanied by headaches, fever, aching joints and vomiting; most victims died less than a week after contracting the disease.

PLAGUE AGAIN

Plague stalked Britain again on a number of occasions during the sixteenth century. In 1563, bubonic plague in London saw 'bills of mortality' return deaths of 1,000 people a week during August, 1,600 in September and 1,800 in October. Many fled from the city: even Queen Elizabeth I moved her court to Windsor Castle, where she ordered the erection of a gallows to swing any person who came there from London. She also blocked the import of goods from the city, all to prevent the spread of plague to her court. In total, about 80,000 people were killed in London by the plague outbreak of 1563 – about a third of the population of the capital at the time.

DROPSY

By the time that Sarah Pickwood, aged forty-nine, died at Norwich in December 1806, she had developed one of the most startling cases of dropsy on record. In the fifty months before her death, she had been 'tapped' thirty-eight times and discharged 350 gallons of fluid, weighing a stunning 4,656lb – or more than 330 stones.

THE END OF CHARLES II

On 2 February 1685, King Charles II was taken to his bedchamber after feeling 'some unusual disturbance in his brain' at Whitehall Palace. He had 16oz of blood drawn from his right arm by two of his physicians. More medical men were rapidly summoned to attend to the King, until a total of fifteen physicians were in attendance; they were led by Sir Charles Scarborough. They decided that the King should be bled of another 8oz of blood by scarification and cupping. He was then administered an emetic to cleanse his stomach and nervous system of impurities. This was supplemented with an enema – twice. His head was also shaved and blistering agents applied.

The King appeared to rally but by evening the doctors were of the opinion that the disordered humours of the King should be thoroughly purged. They administered 'Sacred Bitter Powder' and 'Bryony Compound' – a relative of the cucumber plant that is generally poisonous to humans – as an emetic, purgative and diuretic. Later, a second powder was administered to keep the royal bowels active at night, and another was added to counteract the scalding of his urine caused by the use of blistering drugs. Spirit of 'Sal Ammoniac' (which induces coughing and nausea) was applied to his nostrils to stimulate his brain, and dung plasters applied to his feet. Next morning more purgatives were given, and 10oz of blood was drawn from both jugular veins – and so the round of treatments went on, more antidotes, julep, tonics, powders, Goa Stone, Bezoar Stone. Scarborough recorded 'His Serene Majesty's strength seemed exhausted to such a degree, that the whole assemblage of Physicians lost all hope and became despondent' and Charles 'laid down his mortal crown to take up the Immortal' shortly after noon on 6 February.

THE GARFIELD BULLET

James A. Garfield, twentieth President of the United States, had hardly been in office as President for six months when he was shot from behind in an assassination attempt by Charles Guiteau at Washington DC on 2 July 1881. One shot grazed the President's arm while the other entered his body and lodged somewhere inside.

The President was still alive after the attack – until, that is, his doctors reached him. Medical practice at that time considered that finding the path of the bullet was the priority in the treatment of such a wound. Despite Lister's methods of sterilization being promoted in Britain from the 1860s, most American doctors had not adopted them. Consequently, a number of the physicians treating the President inserted their unsterilized fingers into the wound to probe for the bullet. It remained elusive. A deep bullet wound attracts infection, with the attendant threat of blood poisoning, a situation not helped by all the probing. President Garfield died after suffering a massive heart attack and a ruptured splenic artery aneurysm, following the dual rigours of blood poisoning and bronchial pneumonia, on 19 September 1881.

Tragically, there could have been another chance for Garfield: Alexander Graham Bell had created a metal detector to find the bullet, but as it passed down the President's right side the reading was distorted by the metal springs of the patient's bed. Bell was not allowed to move on to Garfield's left-hand side – where the bullet was finally located during the post-mortem. The device was tried again when away from the President's bed and was found to work well: it would almost certainly have detected the bullet.

NAILED DOWN – LIKE IT OR NOT!

During the cholera epidemics across Britain in the 1840s the sufferers were often removed to temporary cholera hospitals away from population centres. The enormous numbers of patients meant that as soon as a patient died it became imperative to get them out of the bed they had occupied in order to free it for another. The body would then be placed into a wooden 'shell' (a wooden box one could not dignify with the name coffin) and the lid would be nailed or screwed down ready for burial. As there was often a backlog in burials, the shells would often be stacked up outside – and more than one account by those who worked in the temporary hospitals, or by those charged with the burial of the filled shells, tells of kicking or scratching sounds coming from within. The lids were seldom re-opened, however: the employees would grimly state, 'we knew they were going to die anyway.'

SURGEON BARRY'S SECRET

James Barry had a long and distinguished career as a surgeon in the British Army during the first half of the nineteenth century. Serving at a number of locations across the Empire, Barry eventually retired, at the rank of Inspector General in charge of military hospitals, in 1864. After Barry's death from dysentery in 1865, however, an amazing discovery was made: the famous army surgeon was, in fact, a woman.

THE WEIGHT OF THE SOUL

Dr Duncan MacDougall of Haverhill, Massachusetts, weighed a number of terminally sick patients shortly before and after their death on an industrial-sized scale, accurate to the gram. He found an average loss of mass of 21g after death. Upon these findings he based his theory, published in 1907, that the human soul must have a weight of 21g.

A CURE FROM THE DEAD

'To cure wens of fleshy excrescences, pass the hand of a dead body over the part affected on three successive days'; the hand of a suicide or executed murderer was deemed more efficacious than that of one who died a natural death. In the days of public executions, a hangman could occasionally be bribed to allow a sufferer on to the gallows, which saved a bit of time: it enabled the wen to be stroked by the hand of the executed felon while he still swung on the rope.

LEG OFF

An epitaph from St John's churchyard, Chester, reads: 'Under this stone lieth the Broken Remains of Stephen Jones who had his leg cut off without the Consent of Wife or Friends on the 23rd October, 1842, in which day he died. Aged 31 years. Reader I bid you farewell. May the Lord have mercy on you in the day of trouble.'

THE WATTISHAM AFFLICTION

Sixteen-year-old Mary, the daughter of John Wetherset of Wattisham in Suffolk, was taken ill with pains in her leg, foot and toes in January 1762. The following day her entire foot had swollen and black spots appeared on her toes. By the time the blackening reached her knee, the flesh of her leg had putrefied and come off at the ankle – leaving the leg bones bare. Despite the attendance of local surgeons, by April Mary's mother, father, sister and brothers had all watched as their feet simply rotted away. Even their mother's newborn child was seized by the disorder and died. The rest of the family did survive, but no one was ever able to diagnose exactly what had caused 'the Wattisham Affliction'.

PLEASE READ THE INSTRUCTIONS

In 2011 Norfolk pensioner Joy Tomkins had the message 'Do Not Resuscitate' tattooed across her chest, just in case she was involved in an accident or fell ill and attempts were made to revive her. Furthermore, to avoid any confusion she had 'P.T.O' and an arrow tattooed on her back.

NAPOLEON'S WATERLOO

The cause of the death of Napoleon Bonaparte, leader of France, in 1821, has been debated many times, with the direct cause being attributed, originally, to stomach cancer (a statement made by the physician who led his post-mortem). However, later suggestions for the cause include arsenic poisoning, both deliberate and accidental: the theory has it that Napoleon may have ingested the toxin as free-floating particles of the wallpaper in the house where he spent his later years. Recent re-appraisal of the evidence now suggests a peptic ulcer and gastric cancer. In addition to these ailments, 'Boney' was known to suffer from pituitary dysplasia, prolapsed piles, constipation, syphilis, extreme fatigue, colic and cystitis.

5

CRIME AND PUNISHMENT

SERVANT AND MISTRESS

Kate Webster was an Irish con-woman who took up a position as cook and general servant to a widow, Mrs Julia Martha Thomas, at Mayfield Park Villas, Park Road, Richmond, in 1879. Thomas was known for her reputation as a tartar, and this situation proved to be no different. However, she had chosen the wrong woman to annoy, for when Webster was given her notice she flew into such a rage she killed her mistress and then set about disposing of the body. Neighbours would recall 'washing' and 'brushing' sounds coming from the villa, and indeed the washing was hung out. All seemed normal, except for the unusual smell of something strange cooking in the kitchen. A few days later a trunk full of human flesh was washed up by the Thames; a human foot was also found on a nearby dung hill. When Webster started selling, and appearing in, Mrs Thomas's clothes, stern questions about where Mrs Thomas actually was began to be asked. Webster fled to her native Ireland but was soon traced, brought to trial and found guilty of the foul murder. The vital evidence had all been found in the villa – poor Mrs Thomas had been cut up, boiled and burnt on the kitchen and copper grates. The gentlefolks of London no doubt have a little shiver when reading this, even today – how the people who'd purchased some very fine gallipots of meat-dripping, which Webster had been hawking around shortly before she fled, felt is another matter...

TO PRESS FOR AN ANSWER

English courts were in a quandary if suspects refused to plead; if a prisoner pleaded guilty the law stepped in, confiscated their estates and meted out punishment (frequently the death penalty). If they pleaded innocence then a trial would ensue: if found guilty, the prisoner would be punished, and again all possessions were forfeited to the Crown. However, defendants might decide to remain mute – and under old laws would stay unconvicted. It was not until 1827 that silence by a defendant was construed as a 'not guilty' plea. This was a powerful incentive for many not to plead, and thus *peine forte et dure,* otherwise known as pressing, became the law's method of forcing a plea. The victim would be pinioned to the floor of a cell. Minimal sustenance would be given and, over the course of three days, weights were piled upon the chest of the prisoner, leaving him with the agonising choice – plead or die.

BURNING AT THE STAKE

It is a little-known fact that far more women in England were burnt at the stake for breaching the laws of 'petty treason' and 'coining' (counterfeiting coin of the realm) than met the same end in this country for witchcraft. The crime of opening a locked door for a criminal struck at the very heart of the sacred trust between servant and master or mistress. At a time when every household worked along hierarchical lines as a microcosm of the state, with head of the house as King, mistress as Queen and servants as minions, the crimes of killing a husband, or aiding and abetting a criminal to enter a master's house, were classed firmly as 'petty treason'. This crime was punishable by burning at the stake, and this method of execution was only applicable to women. The last woman to be burned at the stake in England was Catherine Murphy, a counterfeiter, in 1789. The penalty of burning at the stake was finally abolished the following year.

AN ACCOUNT OF A BURNING

Eleanor Elsom was executed by burning at Lincoln for the murder of her husband on 20 July 1722. On the day of her execution she was clothed in a cloth 'made like a shift' saturated with tar; her limbs were likewise smeared, and a tar bonnet was placed upon her head. She was brought out of the prison barefoot and, placed upon a hurdle, was drawn upon a sledge to the place of execution, near the gallows. Upon arrival some time was passed in prayer, after which the executioner placed her upon a tar barrel, a height of 3ft, against the stake. A rope ran through a pulley in the stake and was placed around her neck; she herself fixed it with her hands. Three irons also held her body to the stake and, the rope being pulled tight, the tar barrel was taken aside and the fire was lit. It is believed that she was already dead before the flames reached her, as the executioner had pulled on the rope several times whilst the irons were being fixed. The dryness of the wood, and the quantity of tar upon it, saw to it that the fire was exceedingly fierce; the body was to be seen among the flames for some half an hour before it was fully consumed.

IN A BUTT OF MALMSEY WINE

George Plantagenet, 1st Duke of Clarence, was 'privately executed' at the Tower of London on 18 February 1478 on the orders of his brother, King Edward IV. Tradition has it that he was a heavy drinker and was suitably dispatched by being drowned in a butt of Malmsey wine.

THE DEATH OF BUCKINGHAM

George Villiers, 1st Duke of Buckingham, believed by some to have been the lover of James I, and a favoured member of the court of Charles I, had been, at best, an unfortunate military leader. He was planning another campaign, in Portsmouth, when he rose from his bed in August 1628, in 'well-disposed humour', and set off to the Greyhound public house. There, a junior officer named John Felton, who felt aggrieved, believing he had been passed over for promotion, made a thrust at the Duke with 'a common tenpenny knife ... which lighted so fatally, that he slit his heart in two, leaving the knife sticking in the body.' The Duke lived just long enough to cry 'villain', pluck the knife from his chest and make two or three paces towards his killer before he collapsed against a table. Felton was afraid he might be killed in the assassination, and when he was apprehended a note was found pinned in his hat stating his reasons thus:

> That man is cowardly and base and deserveth not the name of a gentleman that is not willing to sacrifice his life for the honour of his God, his King, and his country. Let no man commend me for doing it, but rather discommend themselves as to the cause of it, for if God had not taken away our hearts for our sins, he would not have gone so long unpunished.

While awaiting trial Felton's actions against a courtier despised by many were widely celebrated in verse and on pamphlets, but the law took its course and having been tried and found guilty Felton was hanged at Tyburn on 29 November 1628.

THE ONLY BRITISH PRIME MINISTER TO BE ASSASSINATED

John Bellingham, a merchant broker and export representative, was arrested and imprisoned in Russia after an allegation of fraud. The British Ambassador refused to help him. The original charges were eventually dropped, but during the period of his imprisonment he had incurred severe debts and he was therefore retained behind bars on charges of bankruptcy. After a total of almost six years in prison, Bellingham was finally released and returned to England an embittered man. He wrote numerous letters to politicians and officials explaining his case and seeking compensation, all to no avail; one reply from the Prime Minister's office described Bellingham's claim as 'groundless'. After months of secret preparation, on 11 May 1812 Bellingham took his family to an exhibition of paintings in London, where he casually remarked that he had some business to attend to. He proceeded to the lobby entrance of the House of Commons. At 5.15 p.m. Prime Minister Spencer Percival entered; Bellingham calmly walked forward, fired a single shot that penetrated the Prime Minister's heart and then sat down on a bench. The cry went up of, 'Where is the murderer?' Bellingham replied, 'I am the unfortunate man.' Tried on Wednesday 13 May, Bellingham was found guilty and was sent to the gallows in front of Newgate Prison. His body was delivered to the anatomists, his bones boiled clean and prepared for future use by students. His head disappeared a few years later and was only discovered, after decades, in a box in the cellars of the medical school, some helpful doctor having carefully written 'Bellingham' in ink across the forehead.

NO REST FOR THE WICKED

After the execution of wife-murderer Thomas Weems at the county gaol in Cambridge on August 1819, his body was cut down and conveyed to the Chemical Lecture Room in the Botanical Garden, where Professor Cumming had prepared a powerful galvanic battery. Before an invited and learned audience he performed a number of experiments whereby electric current was passed through various parts of the executed man's body. The results were keenly observed. When galvanic stimulus was applied to the supraorbital nerve (beneath the eye-brow), and the heel, the most extraordinary grimaces were exhibited; 'every muscle in his face was simultaneously thrown into fearful action. Rage, horror, despair, anguish, and ghastly smiles united their hideous expressions in the murderer's face, surpassing the wildest representations of the Fuseli or a Kean [the first a painter of extraordinary Gothic scenes, and the second a famous actor].' The following day the body was opened and placed on public view. No pity for the killer was recorded from the crowds who passed through – just their feelings of 'curiosity, disgust and awe.' The doors were then shut and a large group of learned gentlemen observed an extensive dissection of the body performed by Mr Okes.

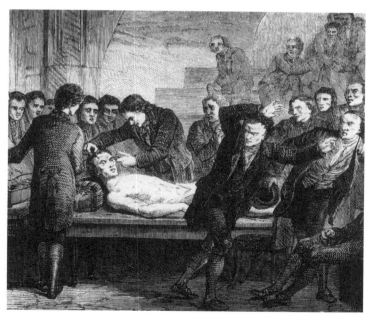

DEATH HEADS

The notion of phrenology, the pseudo-scientific means of ascertaining a person's character by the contours and bumps on the human head, was developed by German physician Franz Joseph Gall in 1796 and became very popular during the nineteenth century. Particular consideration was given to the study of the 'criminal type', and as a consequence many of the notorious murderers of the day had casts taken from their heads after execution. These casts were made into moulds, and plaster reproductions would then be made of them, produced and sold for analysis by (and as example for) the phrenologists and phrenological societies of the day. Conversely, 'death heads' of great men, composers and artists were also made in an attempt to study what could be felt upon their heads to indicate the propensities that made them great.

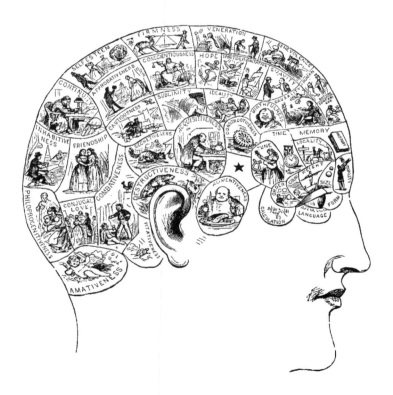

THE 'LAST JUDICIAL BEHEADING' IN BRITAIN

In the annals of crime and punishment it is rare that the execution of the criminal becomes more famous than the crime itself – this is one of those rare exceptions. Robert Goodale, aged forty-five, a man prone to getting drunk and making threats, took one fateful step further and attacked his wife with a billhook. Thinking he had killed her, he put her body down the well at their smallholding on Walsoken Marsh, near Wisbech, where she drowned.

Brought before the assizes at Norwich, he was found guilty and sentenced to death. The date set for his execution was Monday, 30 November 1885. Executioner James Berry observed Goodale was a man of large frame but that he had wasted away while in prison. According to the 'table of drops', Goodale would require 7ft 8in. However, Berry was not happy with this length: Goodale's neck was 'not very muscular', so Berry shortened the drop to 5ft 9in. The surgeon asked Berry if he thought this was enough of a drop to avoid strangulation. Berry assured him that it would be.

On the morning of the execution Goodale was brought onto the gallows and the final preparations were made: Berry pulled the lever, the traps fell open and Goodale was plunged into eternity. Berry recorded what happened next in his memoirs: 'We were horrified, however, to see the rope jerked upwards and for an instant I thought the noose had slipped from the culprit's head or that the rope had broken.' The governor, surgeon and Berry looked into the pit below. Berry continues: 'Having feared the noose had slipped off Goodale's head ... it was worse than that for the jerk had severed the head entirely from the body and both had fallen into the bottom of the pit ... The Governor, whose efforts to prevent any accident had kept his nerves at full strain, fairly broke down and wept.'

Although acquitted of any blame, the 'Goodale Mess' haunted Berry for the rest of his career and probably for the rest of his life. Reporter Charles Mackie recalled the execution when he looked back on his career many years later. With quite some pride he declared he had been present at what could quite justifiably be called 'the last judicial beheading in England.'

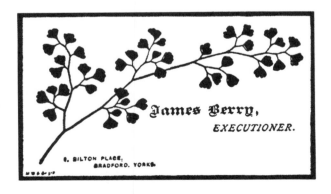

James Berry,

EXECUTIONER.

8, BILTON PLACE,
BRADFORD. YORKS.

THE ONLY ADMIRAL TO FACE
A ROYAL NAVY FIRING SQUAD

On 14 March 1757 John Byng became the only British Admiral to be executed: he met his end before a Royal Navy firing squad. His crime was to have been found guilty, at court-martial, of failing to 'do his utmost' to prevent Minorca falling to the French after the Battle of Minorca during the Seven Years' War.

SMOTHERED SMUGGLERS

Robert Debney and William Cooper were a pair of Suffolk smugglers who devised a well-concealed underground vault for their contraband gin. The entrance was hidden under a heap of horse manure. The pair were hiding from the Excise men inside their vault in June 1778 when they were overcome by the stench-ridden vapours of the dung. They died as a consequence, as their headstone in Tunstall churchyard states:

> Oh think how quickly both these Lives were gone.
> Neither Age nor Sickness brought them to the clay;
> Death quickly took their strength and Sense away
> Both in the Prime of Life they lost their Breath
> And on a sudden were cast down by death.

ILL MET BY MOONLIGHT

A gravestone in the churchyard of Patcham, Brighton, Sussex, records:

Sacred to the memory of Daniel Scales, who was unfortunately shot on Tuesday evening, Nov. 7, 1796.

Alas! swift flew the fated lead,
Which pierced through the young man's head,
He instant fell, resigned his breath,
And closed his languid eyes on death.
And you who to this stone draw near,
Oh! pray let fall the pitying tear,
From this sad instance may we all
Prepare to meet Jehovah's call.

But all is not what the stone would have us believe: in reality, Daniel Scales was a desperate smuggler, who on the night in question, with many more, was coming away from Brighton beach, heavily laden with contraband, when the Excise officers and soldiers fell upon them. The smugglers fled in all directions; a riding officer called upon Scales to surrender his booty, which he refused to do. The officer knew that 'he was too good a man for him, for they had tried it out before', so he shot Scales through the head.

WHODUNNIT?

A stone, dated 1853, in the Minster graveyard, Beverley, is placed to the memory of the victim of a railway carriage tragedy, and bears the following extraordinary inscription:

Mysterious was my cause of Death
In the Prime of Life I Fell;
For days I Lived yet ne'er had breath
The secret of my fate to tell.
Farewell my child and husband dear
By cruel hands I leave you,
Now that I'm dead, and sleeping here,
My Murderer may deceive you,
Though I am dead, yet I shall live,
I must my Murderer meet,
And then Evidence shall give
My cause of death complete.
Forgive my child and husband dear,
That cruel Man of blood;
He soon for murder must appear
Before the Son of God.

HOW DID SHE DO IT?

On 1 January 1886, the wife of Mr Edwin Bartlett found him dead. The doctor was called, and Edwin's father demanded a post-mortem be carried out to explain the sudden death of his healthy son. The post-mortem revealed Edwin had been killed by a large dose of chloroform, traces of which were found in his stomach. The case of 'The Pimlico Poisoning' was to become infamous in the annals of criminal history, and the affair that was revealed between the wife, Mrs Adelaide Bartlett, and Revd George Dyson scandalised Victorian society. Beyond the scandal, the bare facts of the case hinged on how chloroform had been administered: if such a chemical had been given to Edwin Bartlett by force or deception it would have left his throat and digestive passages burnt and inflamed, and there was no evidence of this; the chemical was only found in his stomach. With no evidence presented to show how, or by whom, the chloroform had been administered, Adelaide Bartlett was found not guilty. Sir James Paget commented after the verdict that, 'Mrs Bartlett was no doubt properly acquitted. But now it is to be hoped that, in the interests of science, she will tell us how she did it!' She did not.

PEACEMAKER ON THE GALLOWS

The last triple execution at Newgate was of the murders William Seaman, Albert Milsom and Harry Fowler in 1896. Seaman was convicted of the 'Turner Street Murders' in Whitechapel, while Harry Fowler and Albert Milsom had killed the elderly Mr Henry Smith while attempting to burgle his Muswell Hill home. Both burglars had intended to turn King's Evidence, and the intense animosity between them was apparent – to the extent that Fowler violently attacked Milsom in court. On the gallows Seaman was placed between the two, upon which he exclaimed, 'First time I've ever been a bloody peacemaker!'

HANGING AROUND

As the infamous poisoner Dr William Palmer stepped onto the gallows at Stafford Prison in June 1856, he is said to have looked at the trapdoor and exclaimed, 'Are you sure it's safe?'

The last woman to be executed in public, in Britain, was Frances Kidder, who was hanged at Maidstone on 2 April 1868 for the murder of her step-daughter. The last man to be hanged in public in Britain was Fenian Michael Barrett, who was executed outside Newgate Prison on 26 May 1868 for the bombing at Clerkenwell. Both of these executions were carried out by the nation's longest-serving hangman, William Calcraft, who served as executioner between 1829 and 1874, during which time he carried out an estimated 450 executions.

The last person to be hanged in Wales was Vivian Teed at Swansea on 6 May 1958, for the murder of William Williams, sub-postmaster of Fforestfach post office. The executioner was Robert Leslie 'Jock' Stewart.

The last execution in Northern Ireland was carried out by British executioner Harry Allen in December 1961, when he hanged Robert McGladdery, who had been convicted of the murder of nineteen-year-old Pearle Gamble, at Crumlin Road Gaol in Belfast.

Scotland's last execution was that of Henry John Burnett, carried out by executioner Harry Allen at Craiginches Prison, Aberdeen, on 15 August 1963. Burnett was executed for the murder of seaman Thomas Guyan.

The last woman to hang in Britain was Ruth Ellis, who was executed by Albert Pierrepoint at Holloway Prison, London, on 12 July 1955 for the murder of her lover, David Blakely.

The last executions to be carried out in England and in the United Kingdom were carried out simultaneously on 13 August 1964, when Peter Anthony Allen, at Walton Prison in Liverpool, and Gwynne Owen Evans, at Strangeways Prison in Manchester, were both executed for the murder of John Alan West. The executioners were Harry Allen, who hanged Evans at Strangeways, and Robert Leslie 'Jock' Stewart, who dropped Allen at Walton Gaol.

TEN LAST MEALS ON DEATH ROW, USA

1. Ted Bundy: Serial killer, sent to the electric chair in Florida in 1989. Bundy declined a special meal, so he was given the traditional choice of steak (medium-rare), eggs (over-easy), hash browns, toast, milk, coffee, juice, butter, and jelly.
2. Timothy McVeigh: The 'Oklahoma Bomber', executed by lethal injection in Indiana in 2001. He had two pints of mint-chocolate-chip ice cream.
3. Bruno Richard Hauptmann: Convicted of the Lindbergh kidnapping and murder, he was sent to the electric chair in New

Jersey in 1936. He had celery, olives, chicken, French fries, buttered peas, cherries, and a slice of cake.

4. Danny Rolling: Serial killer known as 'The Gainesville Ripper', executed by lethal injection in Florida in 2006. Lobster tail, butterfly shrimp, baked potato, strawberry cheesecake, and sweet tea.

5. John Wayne Gacy: Serial killer, executed by lethal injection in Illinois in 1994. A dozen deep-fried shrimp, a bucket of original recipe Kentucky Fried Chicken, French fries, and 1lb of strawberries.

6. Ruth Snyder: Murderess, sent to the electric chair in New York in 1928. Chicken parmesan with alfredo pasta, ice cream, two milkshakes, and a twelve-pack of grape soda.

7. Velma Barfield: Multiple murderer, executed by lethal injection in North Carolina in 1984. Declined a special meal, having a bag of Cheez Doodles and can of Coca-Cola instead.

8. Joseph Mitchell Parsons: Murderer, executed by lethal injection in Utah in 1999. Ate three Burger King Whoppers, two large orders of fries, a chocolate shake, chocolate-chip ice cream, and requested a packet of grape-flavoured Hubba-Bubba bubble-gum, to be shared with his brother and a cousin.

9. Ricky Ray Rector: Murderer, executed by lethal injection in Arkansas in 1992. Steak, fried chicken, cherry Kool-Aid and a pecan pie. Rector told the guards who came to escort him to his execution that he had not eaten the pie because he was saving it for later.

10. Thomas J. Grasso: Double murderer, executed by lethal injection in Oklahoma in 1995. Two dozen steamed mussels, two dozen steamed clams, a double cheeseburger from Burger King, half a dozen barbecued spare ribs, two strawberry milkshakes, half a pumpkin pie with whipped cream with diced strawberries and a 16oz can of spaghetti with meatballs, served at room temperature. But Grasso was not pleased with this, and complained that he had requested SpaghettiOs, not spaghetti.

6

SAINTS, DEVILS AND INCORRUPTIBLES

THE INCORRUPTIBLES

There are over 250 'incorruptable' and preserved bodies displayed in Catholic cathedrals and churches worldwide. The following is a list of some of the bodies of the dead who have been preserved miraculously – or with help from embalmers – or have been encased in wax and may still be seen on display in sepulchral glass cases and mausoleums around the world.

St Bernadette Soubirous (1844-1879): The visionary of Lourdes, who died in 1879, is still on display at the Convent of St Gildard, Nevers, France. Her face has been covered by a beautiful representation of it in wax.

Mother Cabrini (1850-1917): This Italian-born nun died in Chicago 1917 and is still on display at Mother Cabrini High School, New York City, USA.

St Rita of Cascia (1381-1457): Calmly bore a stigmata caused by a thorn which fell off a statue of Christ and struck her on the head. It left her with a wound that smelled so badly that the other nuns avoided her. She can be seen at the Basilica of St Rita, Cascia, Italy.

Blessed Margaret of Costello (1287-1320): The body of Blessed Margaret, which has never been embalmed, now lies under the high altar of the church of St Domenico at Citta-di-Castello, Italy.

St Catherine of Bologna (1413-1463): Requested that her body be brought to the cell she used to live in, and that she be kept in a sitting position – and there you will find her, in the same spot that she's been sitting in for 500 years, in the Chapel of the Poor Clares, Bologna, Italy.

St Vincent de Paul (1580-1623): His bones are encased in a wax figure, and rest in a reliquary in the Chapel of the Vincentian Fathers in Paris.

Padre Francisco de Xavier (1506-1552): His incorrupt body now lays in an airtight glass coffin, placed inside a silver casket fashioned by a seventeenth-century Florentine jeweller at the Basilica of Bom Jesus, Goa, India.

Khambo Lama (1852-1927): Buddhist monk who died in the lotus position in 1927. He was exhumed years later and found to still be seated in the position, and remarkably un-decayed, at the Buddist monastery at Ivolginsky Datsari in Siberia, Russia.

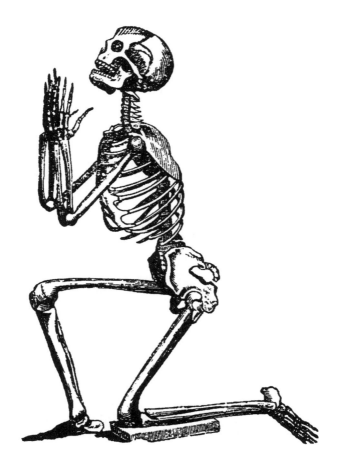

Vladimir Ilyich Lenin (1870-1924): This Russian revolutionary and first Premier of the Soviet Union was embalmed after his death and, with regular maintenance, has been exhibited in Lenin's Mausoleum, Moscow, Russia, ever since.

Chairman Mao Zedong (1893-1976): The body of the leader of the Chinese Revolution was embalmed and is still on display in an ornate mausoleum in Tiananmen Square, Beijing, China. Other Asian communist leaders – such as Kim Il-sung, Ho Chi Minh and, most recently, Kim Jong-il – have all followed in similar style in their own respective mausoleums.

Some other incorruptibles include:

Saint Virginia Centurione Bracelli (1587-1651): Genoa, Italy.
St Catherine Labouré (1806-1876): Chapel, Rue du Bac, Paris, France
Pope John XXIII: St Peter's Basilica, Rome, Italy.
St Clare of Assisi (1194-1253): Basilica di Danta Chiara, Assisi, Italy.
St Silvan (unknown, fourth-century martyr): Church of St Blaise in Dubrovnik, Croatia.
St Zita (1218-1272): Basilica of St Frediano, Lucca, Italy.
Blessed Imelda Labertini (1322-1333): Church of San Sigismondo, Bologna, Italy.
Maria Goretti (1890-1902): Church of Our Lady, Nettuno, Italy.
St John Vianney (1786-1859): The Sanctuaire de St Jean-Marie Vianney (Shrine of St John Vianney) in Ars, Lyon, France.

THE RESTORATION OF PADRE PIO

Padre Pio was a Capuchin monk who came to prominence through his supernatural abilities, said to include: the reading of souls; prophecy; bilocation (being in two places at once); the 'odour of sanctity'; discernment of spirits; and miraculous healings. His most famous spiritual gifts, however, were the stigmata he suffered – the five wounds of Christ – that came to him while praying in 1918 and which he suffered for the rest of his life. Pio died in 1968. His body was exhumed forty years later. It was found to be only partially decomposed upon exhumation. Archbishop Domenico D'Ambrosio described it as being in 'surprisingly good condition ... We could clearly make out the beard. The top part of the skull is partly skeletal but the chin is perfect and the rest of the body is well preserved. The knees, hands and nails are all clearly visible.'

The body of Padre Pio was repaired and preserved for display; his face, which has a very peaceful expression, is coated with a silicon mask, and the top of the skull is covered by the hood of his habit and is still on display at San Giovanni Rotondo, Southern Italy.

PICKED UP HER OWN SEVERED HEAD

Osyth was the daughter of Frithewald and Walburga, the first Christian King and Queen of the East Saxons. After marital strife, she founded a nunnery and eventually became abbess. In around 870 the religious building was attacked by Danish raiders. Osyth attempted to shield her nuns from the raiders, but they cut her head off. Miraculously, however, she picked it up again and walked three furlongs to the church, where she struck the door with her blood-stained hand to indicate that she should be buried there: only then did she fall down and die. The decapitated head of the sainted abbess was kept as a revered relic in a silver casket at St Osyth's Priory, Essex, until the Dissolution, when it disappeared. The spirit of St Osyth is said to walk once a year, head carried in her hands, at the scene of her martyrdom, a holy well in Nun's Wood.

STOLEN BONES

In the year 679 Ely mourned the death of St Etheldreda, foundress and abbess of the monastery at Ely. In the ninth century it was suggested, by the Bishop of Ely, that Withburga, her sainted sister and foundress of the nunnery and church at East Dereham in Norfolk, should lie with her sisters in Ely. However, all at Dereham were vehemently against this. Nonetheless, the Ely monks gave a great feast to the men of Dereham. It was a meal with an ulterior motive, for, as they were preparing to leave, some of their number broke into Withburga's shrine, loaded the coffin onto an ox-wagon and set off for Ely. The desecration of the tomb was discovered the following morning. The men of Dereham set off in pursuit, and caught up with the monks – and the coffin – aboard a barge sailing to Ely. In the *Liber Eliensis*' account, 'the men of Dereham ran along the bank, throwing clods of earth' – but all to no avail. When the Dereham men returned to the town they found the empty tomb had filled with a spring of clear water, a sign of recompense for their lost saint. The well in the churchyard has never run dry, and may still be seen today.

THE WAGES OF SIN

A tale of dubious antiquity tells of how the Devil came to Runwell church in Essex during the middle of a Sunday sermon in about 1250. The elderly vicar, Radulphus, leapt from the pulpit and ran to the church door, pursued by his black enemy, as his parishioners remained frozen in terror in their pews. Radulphus slammed the great door and the Devil, in his haste, was unable to stop. He crashed into the door, leaving his claw marks for all to see. They are there to this day. Radulphus the vicar was, however, never seen again. When the porch was examined, a patch of bubbling sulphurous liquid was found where the vicar was last seen. At the centre of the puddle was a flint that was said to bear a resemblance to the lost cleric. It was removed and reverentially placed in the south wall of the church with an inscription around it: 'The wages of sin is death'.

7

MUMMIES, BOG PEOPLE AND BODY RETENTION

SOME MUMMIES FROM AROUND THE WORLD

The Chinchorro Mummies, found on the Pacific coast of Chile and Southern Peru and dating from about 5000-3000 BC, are the oldest prepared mummified bodies ever found.

Some of the best-preserved natural mummies date from the Inca period in Peru and Chile, some 500 years ago, where children were ritually sacrificed on the summits of mountains in the Andes.

Natural mummies of the Aztec people were frequently displayed in travelling exhibitions, sideshows and museums in the nineteenth century.

Prepared Aztec mummy 'bundles' consist of the remains of the deceased placed in a woven bag or wrap which was often adorned with a ceremonial mask.

Workmen digging an air-raid shelter near the city of Changsha in China in 1971 uncovered an enormous Han Dynasty-era tomb containing over 100 artefacts and the remarkably well-preserved body of Xin Zhui, wife of the Marquis of Han, who died between 178–145 BC.

Mummies discovered in the Tarim Basin in present-day Xinjiang, China, date from 1900 BC to AD 200 and are so well preserved that they can still show some articulation in their joints.

Mahayana Buddhist monks were buried sitting in a lotus position, put into a vessel with drying agents (such as wood, paper, or lime) and surrounded by bricks, with the intention of exhuming them after

three years. These preserved bodies would then be decorated with paint, adorned with gold and put on display in Buddhist shrines.

A female mummy was discovered in 1993 preserved in ice in the sacred Ukok Plateau in the Altay Mountains near the Mongolian border. Dubbed the 'Siberian Ice Maiden', her body was found to have tattoos. She is believed to have been a member of the Pazyryk culture, who lived in the fifth century BC.

The earliest known ancient Egyptian 'mummified' body is the naturally mummified body of an adult man who died more than 5,000 years ago. It was discovered at Gebelein, Egypt.

Twenty naturally mummified bodies were found in Ferentillo, in the Umbrian region of Italy, in 1805. The earliest of these was believed to be some 400 years old.

In Denmark, mummies dating from over 13,000 years BC have been found in various burial mounds, or tumuli.

Eight well-preserved natural mummies who had died about 500 years ago were discovered in a cave at an abandoned Inuit settlement called Qilakitsoq in Greenland in 1972. Among them was the eerily well-preserved body of a six-month-old boy, still in his tiny hooded fur coat.

CURSE OF THE PHARAOHS

The most fabulous tomb to be found, to date, in Egypt's Valley of the Kings was discovered, after years of searching, by Howard Carter in November 1922. It was the tomb of the boy King, Tutankhamun, who had died in 323 BC.

A curious tale associated with the discovery of this tomb was an alleged curse that was said to have been left by the pharaoh to fall upon anyone who violated his tomb. A few months after the entry of the tomb, Lord Carnarvon was bitten on the cheek by a mosquito. The bite became infected and he died in April 1923. At the moment of Carnarvon's death in a Cairo hotel, all the lights of the city went out and, simultaneously, his dog in England let out a great howl and died. A twist to the tale tells of how, when the wrappings of King Tutankhamun were removed from his head, a scab-like depression was found in his left cheek, just like that in Carnarvon's. Newspapers picked up on the story of 'the curse', and by 1929 claims were being made that no less than a dozen people closely connected with the excavation of the tomb had died. Carter dismissed the claims as a 'libellous invention'.

The greatest tragedy of Howard Carter is no myth; although he was a solitary and difficult man, his dedication, talent and contribution to our knowledge of ancient Egypt deserved far more praise. Many looked down upon him because he had not attended a notable school or studied at university. He was never honoured by his county or the many institutions that benefited from his discovery of the tomb of King Tutankhamun. Carter died in 1939. His grave is modestly marked in Putney Vale Cemetery in West London. On his gravestone are inscribed the words from the 'Wishing Cup of Tutankhamun': 'May your spirit live, May you spend millions of years, You who love Thebes, Sitting with your face to the north wind, Your eyes beholding happiness.'

THE TOLLUND MAN

Discovered buried in a peat bog on the Jutland Peninsula in Denmark in May 1950, the Tollund Man's head and face were so well-preserved that, at the time of initial discovery, he was mistaken for a recent murder victim. Subsequent scientific analysis revealed the remains were actually those of a man who had lived and died during the fourth century BC. The cause of his death was hanging: the rope was still around his neck. The original head – and a replica of the body – of the Tollund Man are on display at the Silkeborg Museum in Denmark.

THE HOPE MOOR BOG PEOPLE

'A burial, which turned out to be remarkable in its results, took place on the moors near Hope, in Derbyshire. In the year 1674 a farmer and his female servant, in crossing these moors on their way to Ireland, were lost in the snow, with which they were covered from January to May. Their bodies, on being found, were in such an offensive state that the coroner ordered them to be buried on the spot. Twenty-nine years after their burial, for some reason or other now unknown, their graves were opened, and their bodies were found to be in as perfect a state as those of persons just dead. The skin had a fair and natural colour, and the flesh was soft and pliant: and the joints moved freely, without the least stiffness. In 1716, forty-two years after the accident, they were again examined in the presence of the clergyman of Hope, and were found still in the same state of preservation. Even such portions of dress as had been left on them had undergone no very considerable change. Their graves were about 3ft deep, and in a moist and mossy soil. The antiseptic qualities of moss are well known.' (*Chambers' Book of Days*, 1869)

THE CATACOMBE DEI CAPUCCINI

With bodies dating back to the sixteenth century, these remarkable catacombs in Palermo, Sicily, contain thousands of bodies of men, women and children in a strange state of preservation between mummified and skeletal. Many of the bodies are still dressed in their – now somewhat decayed – clothes, and occupy their own individual niches according to their social status. The last body to be placed in the catacomb was two-year-old Rosalia Lombaro, who died in 1920. Filled with grief, Rosalia's father asked the noted embalmer Alfredo Salafia to preserve her. This he did, and her body appears to be in a remarkable state of preservation to this day: she appears more asleep than dead.

THE MUSEO DE LAS MOMIAS

Founded in 1865, The Museo de las Momias can be found in the little province of Guanajuato in Mexico. A unique local law stipulates that graves in the cemetery have to either be bought for an exorbitant amount or rented every five years. If the deceased's family fails to pay the rent, the body is exhumed and disposed of to make way for new arrivals. Through some mysterious process that scientists have not been able to explain, a small proportion of the bodies from this graveyard end up naturally mummified. Rather than destroying them, the local authorities have these bodies removed to the museum, where they become a part of a vast 'human library' posed in all manner of postures of death.

THE SEDLEC OSSUARY

This small Christian chapel, otherwise known as the 'bone church', located beneath the church of All Saints in Sedlec, a suburb of Kutná Hora in the Czech Republic, contains approximately 40,000 human skeletons, some of which date back to the fourteenth century. The bones came to be there after 1511: they were removed from their graves when the cemetery was enlarged. They remained heaped up here for centuries afterwards. In 1870, František Rint, a woodcarver, was employed by the Schwarzenberg family to put the bone-heaps into order: this he did by stringing skulls and bones into decorative garlands strung across the vaulted ceiling and up the columns of the chapel. He also created further features and decorations using skulls and bones, notably a huge chandelier and the Schwarzenberg coat of arms; this has a bird skeleton pecking at the eye socket of a human skull.

THE CHAPEL OF BONES

The Igreja de São Francisco (Royal Church of St Francis) in Evora, Portugal, is best known for its Capela dos Ossos (Chapel of Bones). It was built by Franciscan monks in the sixteenth century when the bones from numerous monastic cemeteries in Evora were moved to a single consecrated chapel. Seeing an opportunity to contemplate and communicate the inevitability of death, the monks chose to display the bones prominently rather than storing them away – and thus the walls and central pillars of the chapel are literally covered with human skulls and other parts of skeletons from about 5,000 bodies, all held together by cement. In addition to all the bones, there are two full corpses hanging high on a wall. Their identities are unknown, but one popular legend claims they are an adulterous man and his infant son, who were cursed by his jealous wife.

CREEP INTO THE CRYPT

Visitors to the ancient burial chambers under St Michan's church, Dublin, Ireland, can view a number of the dusty corpses in their open coffins. Among these are a nun, a man missing a hand and both feet and a Crusader who had to be sawn in half to fit into his coffin.

COULDN'T LET GO

Joseph Hannath bought the hall at Tydd St Giles, Cambridgeshire, in 1812. He lived there for the rest of his life but his wife predeceased him. He was so heartbroken when his wife died that he kept her body in the house for six weeks before he finally relented and allowed her to be buried. Her ghost is said to walk the house.

JULIA PASTRANA

Julia Pastrana was born into an indigenous Indian tribe in Mexico in 1834 with *hypertrichosis terminalis*, a condition that meant hair grew low down on her forehead – and that she had a beard and pronounced hair growth over large areas of her body. She also had pronounced features and an irregular double set of teeth in both her upper and lower jaw that caused her mouth to project, producing ape-like features. As a result of her unusual appearance she became a sideshow attraction, advertised as a hybrid between an ape and a human – a view, incredibly, endorsed by some medical men, including Dr Alexander Mott who declared her 'the most extraordinary being of the present day' and 'a hybrid between human and orangutan'. Julia married Theodore Lent, the showman who displayed her, and became pregnant. While on tour in Moscow in 1860 Julia gave birth to a child with features akin to her own. Tragically, however, the child did not live above three days and the mother died of postpartum complications a few days later. Lent did not cancel the tour, though: instead, he worked with Professor Sukolov of Moscow University to preserve the bodies of his wife and child and continued to display them in a glass cabinet as the 'Embalmed Nondescript and her child'. Lent was committed to a mental institution in 1884 and the preserved bodies of Julia and her child were sold from show to show and eventually disappeared from public view – until they re-emerged on show in Norway in the 1920s, remaining until the 1970s. In this era they drew yet more attention when an exhibition was

announced in the United States, and a public outcry over the tastelessness of the exhibition arose; as a result, they were again removed from public gaze and put into storage. There the body of the baby was stolen, vandalised and dumped in a ditch and almost completely consumed by mice. Julia now resides in a sealed coffin at the Department of Anatomy in Oslo University and can only be accessed by special permit. In late 2012 the intended burial of Julia's remains was finally announced.

THE NIXONS OF NANTWICH

When a forced entry was made under a bankruptcy order into the house occupied by a Mrs Nixon and her three daughters at Nantwich, Cheshire, in 1926, those who made the entry were in for a shock. They found the girls in the kitchen in terrible physical condition and dressed in rags, one of whom raised her hands and exclaimed: 'We are in God's hands. This is God's House. There is fire and brimstone in every room. Mother must not be touched. She is in God's hands.'

And there was 'Mother', quite dead. She had been so for quite some time, wrapped in a white sheet with food laid out on a table for her. One of the daughters claimed they had not been to bed for five years, choosing to live in the kitchen with their mother instead. The daughters were certified for removal to an asylum.

MUM ON ICE

London sisters Josephine and Valmai Lamas could not bear the thought of burying their mother when she died, at the age of eighty-four, in 1997. Instead, they paid over £15,000 to keep her in a cold storage at a local funeral director's and visited their desiccated mum at least once a week to ensure her make-up was maintained.

'FROZEN DEAD GUY DAYS'

The small mountain town of Nederland, Colorado, holds a most unusual festival based around the frozen corpse of Bredo Morstel. It came about after Norwegian Trygve Bauge had the frozen corpse of his dear departed grandfather brought over as freight with him when he moved to the USA in 1989. The story came to public notice after Trygve outstayed his visa and was deported, leaving his mother,

Aud, to look after the body (which was kept in a freezer in a shed on their property). Public interest was such that the 'Frozen Dead Guy Days' have become an annual local festival, celebrated from Friday to Sunday on the first full weekend of March. The highlights include a coffin race, a slow-motion parade including decorated and classic-car hearses, Frozen Dead Guy lookalike competitions, tours of the newly built shed containing Grandpa Bredo, snow-sculpture competitions, 'polar plunges' into the icy local rivers and even a special 'Frozen Dead Guy' ice cream, which consists of a blue fruit-flavoured ice cream mixed with crushed Oreo cookies and sour gummy worms.

THE FRANKLYN EXPEDITION CREW MEMBERS

On 19 May 1845, 129 men and officers aboard the HMS *Terror* and the HMS *Erebus* set sail from England under the command of Sir John Franklin to explore the Arctic, in the hopes of traversing the final un-navigated section of the Northwest Passage. The expedition was to last three years, but after eighteen months at sea the expedition was lost. Despite many attempts to find out what had happened, nothing was found of them until 1850, when the first relics were discovered – along with the graves of three of the crew members, John Torrington, William Braine, and John Hartnell, on Beechey Island. In 1984 Torrington's body was exhumed by a team led by anthropologist Owen Beattie in an attempt to discover exactly what had caused the deaths of the three, and presumably of the other members of the crew. Torrington was found to be in a remarkable state of preservation: even his eyes were still partially open, his teeth clenched and his lips drawn back in an icy grin.

Two years later the team returned and exhumed the bodies of Hartnell and Braine. Hartnell was also well preserved, but the most startling of all the bodies was that of Braine, whose face had been covered by a bright red handkerchief: when it was removed, they were greeted by a grinning mouth and a flattened nose – the coffin had not been quite deep enough, and the coffin lid had pressed into Braine's nose when it was sealed. Although his eyeballs weren't well preserved, his half-opened eyes made him look as if he had just woken from a long nap.

The findings of the post-mortem examinations revealed high levels of lead in all three crew members, caused by the tins that contained the food the expedition had relied upon. Lead poisoning had not killed them, but it had weakened them and left them vulnerable to exposure and disease.

THE CONQUEROR OF EVEREST?

Mountaineer George Mallory could have been the first man to stand on top of Mount Everest when he led an expedition there in 1924. Unfortunately, however, he did not make it back down again to claim his prize. What had happened to him remained a mystery until his wind-dried, frozen (but well-preserved) remains were found on the North Face, at about 26,000ft up, seventy-five years later, in 1999. He was discovered lying face down. Much of the back of his body had become exposed, but his hobnail boots were intact and his underside still retained most of his layers of clothing: tweed suit, jumpers, thermal underwear and shirt bearing the name tag 'George Mallory'. His pockets were also found to contain a number of his personal effects, including his goggles, a tube of zinc oxide, an altimeter, letters – and even a box of Swan Vesta matches. But still there was no direct evidence to confirm or deny whether he had reached the summit before his death, so his place in history cannot be confirmed.

FROZEN SOLDIERS

The bodies of three Austrian soldiers were discovered over 11,000ft up the San Mateo Mountains in Italy in 2004. All three bodies had been preserved in the mountain ice, as had their uniforms and the equipment found with them. It was believed that they had been killed by a grenade during a battle in September 1918, and that their bodies had lain there, undetected, ever since.

DEAD... BUT NOT BURIED

Martin van Butchell used eccentric behaviour, dress and gimmicks to publicise his business as a surgeon and dentist in the 1760s. His most infamous stunt followed the death of his wife. He consulted doctors about preserving her body in the most life-like way, which they did, to the best of their ability, using a pair of 'nicely matched glass eyes' and injections of preservatives that contained colouring to give Mary's cheeks a fine rosy glow. She was then put on display within a glass-topped coffin with curtains. She was a great draw for trade, but when he remarried the new Mrs van Butchell was not so keen to have her hanging around and the body was given to Dr John Hunter for his museum.

DON'T CRY FOR ME

In 1952, the corpse of Eva 'Evita' Perón, First Lady of Argentina from 1946 until her death, was embalmed by Dr Pedro Ara. He began the process within hours of her death. Accounts of people who later saw and touched Eva's embalmed corpse marvelled at its life-like quality and softness. Ara was meticulous in his work and it took a year to embalm the body completely, at a cost to the government of a reported $100,000. A military coup led to her body being hidden from public view at a number of locations in Buenos Aires and then being smuggled out of Argentina to Italy, in secret, in 1957, where she was buried, under a false name, in 'lot 86, garden 41', at Musoco Cemetery, Milan. The situation in Argentina changed again and Eva's body was then removed to Juan Perón's exiled home in Spain in 1971. Juan Perón returned to Argentina in 1973 but died suddenly the following year. However, his third wife, Isabella, oversaw the return of Evita's body to Argentina, where it was restored and briefly put on display for the public to visit. Finally, Eva was returned to her family's mausoleum in the Recoleta Cemetery, Buenos Aires, in 1976, where she lies, 5m down, in a solidly erected crypt with two security doors to ensure Eva now rests in peace.

HUNTER GETS HIS MAN

Charles O'Brien (also known as Byrne) was a giant of a man who stood a massive 7ft 8in tall. He earned a living by exhibiting himself at shows, theatres, public rooms and pubs but certainly did not fancy that life as an eternal fate for his bones. Often men and women of great height do not have long lives, and O'Brien certainly did not help himself in this respect with his excessive drinking – he fell grievously ill when he was still in his early twenties. The scouts for the anatomist Dr John Hunter were circling like vultures, but O'Brien was determined to foil them, leaving strict instructions that after death his body be watched, day and night, until a lead coffin was made and his body could be taken out to the Downs for burial in a lake in 20 fathoms of water. O'Brien died, at the age of twenty-two, in 1783, while staying in Cockspur Street, Charing Cross, London.

Hunter was not to be dissuaded and met with those charged to watch over the giant's body to see if they could 'reach an understanding'. As the drink flowed, the deal was discussed; the cost was high, and some accounts state that a sum of between £500 and £700 was paid to secure the body. Sure enough, the weighted

coffin of O'Brien was buried with due ceremony in the waters, as promised, but Hunter had his body and the skeleton of an un-named giant went on display in his museum.

JIMMY GARLICK

In 1839 a group of workmen carrying out excavations under the chancel of the church of St James, Garlickhythe, on Upper Thames Street, London, were shocked to discover the well-preserved body of a man who had been interred there centuries before. There was no clue as to who he was but it has been suggested that he could well have been one of the six early Lord Mayors of London buried in the church. For want of a positive identification, the body was soon given the pseudonym 'Jimmy Garlick' and was preserved in a glass-fronted coffin in the vestibule of the church with the legend, 'Stop, stranger, stop as you pass by. As you are now, so once was I. As I am now, you soon will be, so pray prepare to follow me,' displayed at his feet.

A GLIMPSE, THEN GONE FOREVER

After being captured at the Battle of Preston, James, 3rd (and last) Earl of Derwentwater, was executed on Tower Hill, London, in February 1716 for his part in the Jacobite uprising. In October 1874 his body was taken to the chapel at Thorndon Hall, Ingrave, Essex, and re-interred. Dr Earle of Brentwood was present when the coffin was opened for identification, and his daughter recorded what her father had witnessed:

> The body was in three coffins. First, an oak one. Then one covered with crimson velvet and then a leaden one. When the lid was raised they looked on the perfect face and figure of a young and very handsome man fully dressed with a lace cravat bound tightly round his neck. And even as they looked he was not: face and figure faded before their eyes and in its place a skeleton; the air had done its work, and they asked each other had they really seen this very man, dead for over 150 years.

THE MUMMY AT THE FAIRGROUND

Elmer McCurdy (1880-1911) was an outlaw in the American West who was killed in a gunfight shortly after he screamed, 'You'll never take me alive!' His body was taken to a funeral home in Oklahoma but no one claimed the corpse so the undertaker embalmed it and allowed people to see it for a nickel a time. Five years later, a man presented himself to the undertaker purporting to be Elmer's long-lost brother and claimed he wanted to give the corpse a decent burial. Within two weeks, however, Elmer was a featured exhibit with a travelling carnival and from that time on, for the next sixty years, Elmer's body was sold to a succession of wax museums, carnivals, and haunted houses.

Elmer's body ended up at the 'The Laff in the Dark' funhouse at the Long Beach Pike amusement park in California, but by that time the true story of the embalmed corpse had been forgotten. During filming of the television series *The Six Million Dollar Man* at the amusement park in 1976 a crew member was moving what everyone believed was just a macabre fairground mannequin when the arm broke off and the mummified human remains were revealed. Investigations soon revealed the truth, and outlaw Elmer McCurdy was finally buried in the Boot Hill section of the Summit View Cemetery in Guthrie, Oklahoma, on 22 April 1977.

THE BODY OF MR BENTHAM

The eminent philosopher Jeremy Bentham had spent years contemplating how dead bodies might be used for the good of society. When he died in June 1832, Bentham was preparing a pamphlet entitled *Auto-Icon; or Farther Uses of the Dead to the Living*. In the paper, Bentham suggested people could be preserved to become their own memorials, exhibited in suitable places, such as family homes, or varnished to protect them from the elements in gardens as ornaments. He went on to suggest that even the smallest of homes could have auto-icons, with preserved heads displayed in cabinets. Although Bentham's ideas did not catch on, his own last wishes were carried out and the process was attempted upon his own body. Today he is in University College London (the college he helped to found) in a large display case, preserved and dressed in his own clothes with a few of his favourite objects around him (although his head has been replaced with a fine wax likeness). His actual head was found when he was given a clean and smarten up in 1898; it was wrapped in tarred cloth in his rib cage. Attempts to preserve his actual head had apparently failed and it had become dark, leathery and more like a zombie than an icon. For some time the head was displayed between the feet of the great man, with the startling blue glass eyes he had chosen in life for his icon looking eerily out at all who passed.

CHAPTER EIGHT

CELEBRITY BODY PARTS

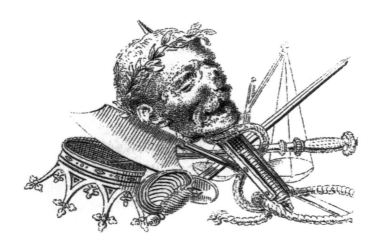

CROMWELL'S HEAD

After his death in 1658, Oliver Cromwell was buried in Westminster Abbey, near his old compatriots Henry Ireton and John Bradshaw. After the restoration, Charles II wreaked revenge on those who committed treason against his father. On 26 January 1661 the bodies of 'regicides' Cromwell, Ireton and Bradshaw were unceremoniously disinterred and on 30 January, the twelfth anniversary of his father's execution, they were drawn on a sledge to Tyburn.

There their bodies were hanged until sundown, when they were all beheaded. The heads were then parboiled and, covered in pitch, were impaled on spikes at Westminster Hall on the anniversary of Charles I's funeral. Cromwell's head remained there for over twenty years until it was brought down in a gale and was picked up by a sentry. After passing through a number of hands and being exhibited in various curiosity shows, the head was given by the niece of the last show's proprietor to her family doctor, Dr Josiah Henry Wilkinson, for safe-keeping. She eventually sold it to him. Passing down the family line to Canon Horace Wilkinson of Woodbridge, during the 1930s, the head, still on its iron spike and with its fragment of wooden pole, was scientifically examined and revealed evidence of the eight axe blows used to remove Cromwell's head, his 'reddish hair' and even 'the historical wart which Cromwell insisted on his portrait painters putting in'. The nose had been flattened during the beheading; almost all the teeth were gone, and the lips were broken to fragments, but all the tests proved conclusively this was indeed the head of Oliver Cromwell. Canon Wilkinson believed Cromwell's head was given a fitting final resting place: he presented it to Cromwell's old edifice of learning, Sidney Sussex College, Cambridge. The head resides there to this day in a secret location known only to a few staff.

THE HEAD OF THE DUKE OF SUFFOLK

In 1849 a well-preserved head was found in the vaults of Holy Trinity church, built on the site of the old Grey family chapel. It was assessed by Dr Mouat:

> [That it was] belonging to a man past the prime of life and that the head was removed by rapid decapitation during life admits no doubt. A large gaping gash, which had not divided the subcutaneous structures, shows that the first stoke of the axe was misdirected … The reaction of the skin, the violent convulsive action of the muscles, and the formation of a cup-like cavity with the body of the spinal bone at the base, prove that the severance was effected during life and in cold weather.

Sir George Younghusband expanded on this in *Tower of London*:

> There was no shrinkage of the face, the eyes are wide open, and the eyeballs and pupils perfectly preserved, though of parchment colour. The skin all over is of the same yellowish hue. When first found, the hair of the head and beard were still on, but owing to its very brittle state and from being handled by several people, these broke off.

Examined by Sir George Scharf, Keeper of the National Portrait Gallery, it was confirmed that the features corresponded to those in contemporary portraits of Henry Grey, Duke of Suffolk, who had been executed two days after his daughter, Lady Jane Grey, in February 1554. It was recorded that it had taken two blows of the axe to decapitate the Duke on the cold morning of his execution.

RICHARD II'S JAWBONE

In 1766 the tomb of Richard II (1367-1400) in Westminster Abbey had fallen into such a state of disrepair that a lad stuck his hand through a crack and pulled out the King's jawbone. One of the boy's older companions scolded the boy and confiscated the bone. It remained in his family until 1906, when one of his descendants returned it to the Dean and the bone was restored to the tomb.

THE HOLY PREPUCE

Otherwise known as the Holy Foreskin of Jesus Christ, removed during his circumcision, this is a holy relic that has been known for centuries. One of the earliest recorded sightings of it was on 25 December 800, when Charlemagne gave it to Pope Leo III after his coronation. As time passed, a number of religious houses claimed ownership: indeed, as many as eighteen locations all claimed they displayed the Holy Foreskin during the Middle Ages! In 1900, the arguments were still rumbling on and the Roman Catholic Church resolved the dilemma by ruling that anyone thenceforward writing or speaking of the Holy Prepuce would be excommunicated.

A VERTEBRAE OF CHARLES I

The fourth cervical vertebra and part of the beard of King Charles I (executed by beheading in 1649) was retained by Sir Henry Halford, physician to George III and President of the Royal College of Surgeons, as a small souvenir of the exhumation of the King's remains at Windsor in April 1813. The remains were kept in a special box by Halford and the vertebrae, cleft by the axe, was often passed around the noble surgeon's dinner table as a curiosity. After the death of Halford, his grandson decided that they should be returned to the royal family and saw that the relics were returned to the hand of the Prince of Wales. With Queen Victoria's permission the relics were replaced in the coffin of King Charles I in December 1888.

GOYA'S HEAD

When the remains of Francisco Goya (1746-1828), the Spanish artist known for his dark subject matters, were exhumed from a chapel in Bordeaux, France, for reburial in his native country in November 1888 his head was found to be missing. It is believed it had been removed before – or shortly after – his interment, for phrenological study.

A PLACE FOR THE HEART

When writer and statesman Sir William Temple died at Moor Park, Farnham, Surrey, in 1699, he left instructions: 'his heart [was] to be enclosed in a silver case or earthenware basin and buried under the sundial, over against a window from whence he used to contemplate the works of God after he had retired from worldly business.'

NAPOLEON'S PENIS

People have been fixated on Napoleon's penis since his doctor allegedly removed it during his autopsy and gave it to a priest in Corsica in 1821. The penis, which was not properly preserved, went on display in Manhattan in 1927, when it was described in *TIME* magazine as looking akin to a 'maltreated strip of buckskin shoelace'. First put up for auction by Christie's in 1972, the member was observed to be approximately 1in long and was listed as 'a small dried-up object'. Failing to make its reserve, it was purchased a few years later by a New Jersey urologist for $3,800. After his death his daughter inherited the shrivelled member and claims to have received at least one offer of $100,000 for it.

SHAKE – FOR OLD TIME'S SAKE

In 1793 Philip Thickness, formerly of London but then residing in Bologna, left direction in his will that, after his death, his right hand be cut off and sent to his son, Lord Audley, 'in hopes that such a sight may remind him of his duty to God, after having so long abandoned the duty he owed to a father who once affectionately loved him.'

THE HANDS OF JUAN PERÓN

Popular Argentinian President Juan Perón (1895-1974) was buried in La Chacarita Cemetery in Buenos Aires, but thirteen years later his body was desecrated by grave robbers, who sawed off his hands and sent government officials a demand for an $8 million ransom for their return.

THOMAS HARDY'S HEART

When the great author and poet Thomas Hardy died in 1928, the directions in his will clearly stated that he wished to be buried unostentatiously in the churchyard at Stinsford, deep in his beloved Wessex. However, his executors were offered the chance to bury him in Westminster Abbey. A compromise was reached with his widow: the body would be buried in the abbey, but his heart must return to Stinsford. A surgeon, accompanied by Hardy's family doctor, removed the heart: it was wrapped in a hand towel and placed – for want of a better receptacle – in a biscuit tin. The doctor then took it to his own house, ready for transfer to the burial casket the following day. One story, which has yet to be conclusively dismissed, is that during that night the tin containing the heart was knocked over by the doctor's family cat, which ate the heart. It was replaced in secret, according to the tale, with one from an animal.

THE BRAIN AND EYES OF EINSTEIN

The brain of genius Albert Einstein (1879-1955) was removed and preserved just seven hours after his death by pathologist Thomas Stoltz Harvey. This was only revealed by journalist Steven Levy in 1978: he discovered that the brain sections, still in the possession of Harvey, had been preserved in alcohol, in two large mason jars within a cider box, for over twenty years. Whether Einstein had given permission for this to happen after his death is still a matter of dispute. Stolz also gave permission to Einstein's ophthalmologist, Dr Henry Abrams, to remove the eyes. The eyes remain suspended in formaldehyde in a glass vial in a New Jersey bank vault, and despite media hype in the 1990s – which claimed he was hoping to auction them off, for which figures of $5 million were bandied around – Adams has reassured reporters that he has no intention of selling them.

ELVIS'S WART

The only major remnant of the body of Elvis Presley, outside of his grave, is the wart removed from his right wrist in 1958. Kept in a jar of formaldehyde, it is now one of the 30,000 Elvis items in Joni Mabe's 'Panoramic Encyclopedia of Everything Elvis' on display at the Loudermilk Boarding House Museum in Cornelia, Georgia, USA. She also has a toenail that possibly belonged to Elvis, which she plucked out of a carpet on a visit to Graceland.

HAYDN'S HEAD

Shortly after his death in 1809, the head of the great composer Joseph Haydn was obtained by phrenologists. They bribed the sexton to take it from his grave in Hundsturm Cemetery, Vienna. The skull was left, in a will, to the Society of the Friends of Music – and there it remained for many years. In 1932, Prince Paul Esterházy built a marble tomb for Haydn in the Bergkirche in Eisenstadt with the express purpose of reuniting the composer's remains but there were many further delays, and it was only in 1954 that the skull was finally transferred from the Society of the Friends of Music to this tomb.

RA-RA RASPUTIN,
LOVER OF THE RUSSIAN QUEEN

Mystic Grigori Yefimovich Rasputin attracted much attention – and many lovers – in pre-revolution Russia. Much gossip was attached to his influence in the court of the Tsar and – notably – to his influence over the Tsarevich Alexei and the boy's mother, Tsarina Alexandra. Rasputin was murdered by Prince Felix Yusupov and a number of other assassins in December 1916. According to an account given by Rasputin's daughter Maria, they attacked the mystic after unsuccessfully poisoning him with food and wine laced with arsenic. Yusupov fired a shot at Rasputin's head, but only wounded him. He fired again and again, but the mystic was seen to struggle to get up; the assassins then clubbed him to the ground. As Rasputin fell, another young nobleman pulled out a dagger and castrated him, flinging the severed penis across the room. His body was then wrapped in a carpet and thrown into the river, where his dead body was recovered a few days later. One of Yusupov's servants recovered the severed organ and handed it over to a maid, who had been one of Rasputin's lovers, and she, in turn, fled with it to Paris – where she kept it in a polished wooden box, 18in by 6in in size, on top of her bedroom bureau. It remained there for years afterwards – or at least that is one story. In 2004, it was claimed that Rasputin's penis is displayed at the first Russian museum of erotica in St Petersburg. The institution was founded by Igor Knyazkin, the chief of the prostate research centre at the Russian Academy of Natural Sciences, who claims that he bought it from a French antiquarian for $8,000. This member had turned up in 1999, when a small box containing 'some mummified hairy shrunken object' was found in an abandoned house in a Parisian suburb that used to belong to Akilina Laptinskaya, Rasputin's secretary. The 12in-long member was painstakingly rehydrated and restored and is now displayed in preservation fluid in a glass specimen jar. However, a rumour still persists that this whole affair may be a clever hoax.

THE LAST BITS OF HITLER

Officials at Russia's Federal Archives Service and at the Russian Federal Security Service, or FSB, the main successor of the KGB, claim the jawbone and a 4in fragment of cranium – with a hole where a bullet appears to have exited through the left temple – which were recovered from a crudely burnt corpse in a ditch outside the Führerbunker in 1945, and still in their possession, are the only surviving remains of Nazi leader Adolf Hitler.

GERONIMO!

Geronimo, the feared Native-American fighting man and leader of the Bedonkohe Apache, died while in US captivity at Fort Sill, Oklahoma, in 1909. A story has become attached to the fate of his bones: the tale relates how six members of the elite Yale University Skull and Bones secret society (including Prescott Bush, grandfather of 43rd President George W. Bush) allegedly dug up Geronimo's grave while serving as army volunteers in Oklahoma during the First World War. Despite lawsuits demanding the return of the remains and repeated denials of ownership from the present members of the Skull and Bones, it is rumoured that the skull still makes an appearance at their nocturnal initiation rites.

MUSSOLINI'S BRAIN

Wartime Italian Fascist leader Benito Mussolini was summarily executed by partisans and hung upside down on a meat hook, with his mistress and others, in the Piazzale Loreto in Milan in April 1945. Mussolini's body was then buried in an unmarked grave in the Musocco Cemetery but this was located by a group of neo-Fascists in 1946, and they made off with the remains of their hero. The body was 'recaptured' later that same year. Unsure what to do with it, the authorities held the remains for ten years before agreeing to allow them to be re-interred at Mussolini's birthplace of Predappio in Romagna. However, not all of Mussolini made it to this grave: his brain was not intact and in 1966 – when part of the brain was returned to his widow – it was revealed that the US had obtained a significant part of it for medical study. A further forty-three years later, Mussolini's granddaughter Alessandro tipped off police that someone was selling glass vials alleged to hold the remaining brains and blood of Mussolini on eBay for €15,000. The company promptly removed the listing.

SOUVENIRS FROM THE GALLOWS

After murderer Joshua Slade was executed upon the Huntingdon Gallows in 1827, his body was handed to the anatomists. His skin was flayed from his corpse, tanned and sold as grim souvenirs, and his skeleton displayed in a travelling show. In like style, a copy of *An Authentic and Faithful History of the Mysterious Murder of Maria Marten* by James Curtis was bound in the skin of her murderer, William Corder, taken from his body and tanned by West Suffolk Hospital surgeon George Creed. He also preserved and kept Corder's scalp, with the right ear still attached.

MIRACULOUS HEADS

John Fisher, Bishop of Rochester, was beheaded on Tower Hill, London, in 1535 for denying that Henry VIII was the supreme head of the English Church. The decapitated head was parboiled and impaled upon a pole on London Bridge. For the next twelve days it was said that the Bishop's head grew fresher and ruddier, to the degree that the head appeared to be in a more healthy state that when it was attached to his body. People began to talk of miracles. Henry decided that this was embarrassing, and ordered it be taken down at night and cast into the river.

After his execution on Tower Green in 1535, meanwhile, Thomas More's head was placed on a pole upon London Bridge. More's eldest daughter, Margaret Roper, resolved to end this ignominious display by obtaining it. According to Aubrey she implored God in prayer: 'That head has lain many a time in my lap, would to God it would fall into my lap as I pass under.' Her wish was miraculously granted and the head did indeed fall as she passed. News of the incident reached the authorities who suspected she had bribed the bridge keeper to obtain the head for her. She was imprisoned but was soon liberated and was allowed to keep her father's head, which she had enclosed in a leaden box, and preserved it with tender devotion. When she died in 1544 she asked that her father's head be buried with her.

RALEIGH'S HEAD

After his execution in Old Palace Yard in 1618, the decapitated head of Sir Walter Raleigh was shown on either side of the scaffold. It was then put into a leather bag, over which Sir Walter's gown was thrown, and the whole lot conveyed away in a mourning coach by Lady Raleigh. Her ladyship kept the head in the bag with her for the rest of her life, some twenty-nine years. This tradition was equally observed by their loyal son Carew, with whom the head was believed to have been buried upon his death.

RESTING IN PEACE?

John Milton, the author of *Paradise Lost*, was laid to rest in the church of St Giles, Cripplegate, after his death from consumption in 1674. A story handed down since the late eighteenth century tells of how, in 1790, Milton's bones were scurrilously disinterred, and hanks of his hair torn off – and his teeth knocked out – and carried off by the churchwardens to give, or sell, as keepsakes for Milton fans. Elizabeth Grant, their female gravedigger, even used to 'keep a candle' and would, for a small remuneration (of about three pence), take visitors into the undercroft to see the mutilated remains.

THE UNIQUE WILLIAM BUCKLAND

Professor William Buckland (1784-1856) was a notable academic, geologist and palaeontologist with a sense of adventure and a keen eye for the strange and the anomalous. He claimed that he had eaten his way around most of the animal kingdom and shared the accounts of his gastronomic exploits with his many friends. The writer and raconteur Augustus Hare recorded what has become Buckland's most infamous incident, which occurred when he was a guest at dinner at a country house: 'Talk of strange relics led to mention of the heart of a French King, (Louis XVI) preserved at Nuneham in a silver casket. Dr Buckland, while looking at it, exclaimed, "I have eaten many strange things, but have never eaten the heart of a King before," and before anyone could prevent him, he had gobbled it up and the precious relic was lost forever.'

Buckland died on 14 August 1856, but he had one last jest left. The time came to dig his grave. The plot was especially chosen, and paid for in advance, by the good professor – with mischief in mind! As the sexton set his spade to the ground, he soon discovered an outcrop of solid Jurassic limestone just a few inches below the surface. Despite their best efforts with pick and shovel, it proved impossible to excavate the plot with those tools: explosives eventually had to be used to excavate the grave. Richard Whatley's *Elegy for Buckland*, written in 1820, says:

Where shall we our great
Professor inter
That in peace may rest his bones?
If we hew him a rocky sepulchre
He'll rise and break the stones
And examine each stratum that lies around

For he's quite in his element
underground.

TO KISS A QUEEN

The tomb of Queen Catherine de Valois, who died in 1437, was
removed from her original chapel of rest after Henry VIII demolished
it to make room for his own chapel. Her coffin was left by the side of
her husband's tomb for the next 300 years. Among a number of people
who were shown her remains was diarist Samuel Pepys, who recorded
the moment in 1669: 'I had the upper part of her body in my hands,
and I did kiss her mouth, reflecting upon it that I did kiss a Queene.'

LOCAL CELEBRITY BODY PARTS

Coming from a generation where tequila containing worms was
a popular novelty drink, I can certainly confirm that a far more
revolting ingredient than that is used in the Sour-Toe Cocktail, a
unique drink served in the Downtown Hotel, Dawson City, in the
Yukon territory of Canada. The original toe of Sour-Toe fame
belonged to a trapper and miner named Louie Liken. Liken did not
trust doctors and, fearing the onset of gangrene in an injured big
toe, had the digit amputated by his brother with an axe. The toe
was kept as a souvenir for years. It was eventually found in their
cabin, when it was cleared, by Captain Dick Stevenson. Conferring
with friends, he incorporated the toe in a cocktail and a drinking
challenge was established in 1973. The original rules were that the
toe must be placed in a beer glass full of champagne, and that the toe
must touch the drinker's lips during the consumption of the alcohol
before he or she can claim to be a true 'Sourtoer.'

The drinking challenges with the original toe came to an abrupt
end when a guy tipped backwards, after his thirteenth glass, and
swallowed the toe. It was not recovered, but a number of others
have been donated in its stead by people who've lost them through
accident or amputation. The rules have changed a little over the
years. Today, the Sour-Toe can be had with any drink, but one rule
remains the same – the drinker's lips must touch the toe. As the
saying goes, 'You can drink it fast, you can drink it slow – but the
lips have gotta touch the toe!'

In January 1925 a woman's leg, complete with laced boot and
stocking, was handed in to the Essex Police at Ongar. It was

discovered by local motor-mechanic Mr W. Lane, who had been travelling through Stanford Rivers on his motorbike at night when he felt a disconcerting bump under his wheels. He stopped, went back to investigate and discovered the limb. A search conducted immediately after the grim discovery failed to discover the rest of the body; as far as the leg was concerned, a contemporary newspaper report in the *Weekly Dispatch* concluded, 'so far no one has come forward to claim it'.

Sixty-five-year old grandmother Uta Schneider of Stuttgart, Germany, was beside herself when her beloved husband of thirty-five years, Heinrich, died in hospital in 2006. She wanted to keep something of him as a souvenir, so she cut off his penis, wrapped it in foil and placed it in a lunch box. She then set off to return home with it, where she intended to preserve it. However, a suspicious nurse alerted the police, who arrested Mrs Schneider. She defended her actions by claiming, 'It was his best asset and gave me so much pleasure. I wanted to pickle it for eternity. He would have wanted it. We called it his joystick. I wanted it to remember him by.'

9

THAT'S ENTERTAINMENT

SOME DRAMATIC FINAL CURTAINS

French playwright Jean-Baptiste Poquelin, better known by his stage name of Molière, collapsed on stage in a fit of coughing and haemorrhaging while performing in the last play he'd written – *Le Malade Imaginaire* ('The Hypochondriac') in 1673. Molière insisted on completing his performance, after which he collapsed again. He died a few hours later.

Composer Jean Baptiste Lully was beating time by banging a long staff (a precursor to the bâton) against the floor, as was the common practice at the time, while conducting a *Te Deum* in honour of Louis

XIV's recent recovery from illness in 1687. Unfortunately, Lully accidentally struck his toe. The resulting injury created an abscess that turned gangrenous: refusing to have his toe amputated, the gangrene spread and killed him.

Restoration dramatist Thomas Otway, best known for *Venice Preserv'd, or A Plot Discover'd* (1682), was by 1685 in 'reduced circumstances' and had no other option than to beg for bread on Tower Hill, London. A passer-by, learning who he was, gave Otway a guinea and the playwright dashed off to a baker's shop – but tragically, in his haste, he did not chew his first bite properly and he choked to death.

Austrian conductor Felix Mottl suffered a heart attack while conducting Wagner's *Tristan and Isolde*. He died eleven days later, on 2 July 1911.

Stage magician Chung Ling Soo (real name William Ellsworth Robinson) became famous for his 'bullet catch', whereby he would face a firing squad and catch the missiles. In March 1918 he was appearing at the Wood Green Empire, London, when the trick mechanism of the gun went wrong and it actually fired the bullet. It hit Soo in the chest. A master of characterisation, many people believed he was Chinese: it was only when he was hit by the bullet that he allowed his persona to drop, crying 'Oh my God! Something's happened. Lower the curtain!' He died in hospital the following day.

American film actress Martha Mansfield died in 1923 after sustaining severe burns on the set of the film *The Warrens of Virginia* after a smoker's match, tossed away by a cast member, ignited her Civil War costume of hoopskirts and ruffles.

One of circus strongman Zishe (Siegmund) Breitbart's special talents was to drive a spike through five 1in-thick oak boards using only his bare hands. While demonstrating this feat in 1925 he accidentally pierced his knee: the rusty spike caused an infection that resulted in fatal blood poisoning.

A seventy-nine-year-old noted London Professor of Music named Nicola Coviello was taken to Coney Island by a nephew he was visiting in 1926. Among the entertainments was a jazz band. The old professor listened for a few minutes to the band playing at a furious pace; he had never heard anything quite like it. He then turned to his nephew declaring, 'That isn't music. Stop it!' He appeared to sway – and then he dropped down dead on the spot.

Vaudeville performer John 'Chuck' O'Connor died of a heart attack while dancing on stage in his family act in 1927.

In 1931, English novelist Arnold Bennett drank a glass of water in a Paris hotel to prove the water was safe. He died two months later from the typhoid he contracted.

Albert Stoessel died of a heart attack while on stage conducting an orchestra for the American Academy of Arts and Letters in New York on 12 May 1943.

Blues star Johnny Ace became drunk and shot himself in the head during a break in his performance at Houston, Texas, in 1954. Witnesses stated Ace had been waving the revolver around the table and someone said, 'Be careful with that thing.' He replied, 'It's okay! Gun's not loaded … see?' He pointed it at himself, with a smile on his face, and pulled the trigger.

Matinee idol Tyrone Power, famed for his performances in such films as *The Mark of Zorro* (1940) and *The Black Swan* (1942), suffered a heart attack while filming a sword fight with co-star George Sanders for the film *Solomon and Sheba* on 15 November 1958. He died en route to hospital.

British actor Gareth Jones was portraying a character who died of a heart attack in a live television broadcast of the science-fiction play *Underground* in the ITV series *Armchair Theatre* when he died of a real heart attack between his scenes on 30 November 1958. The actors and director improvised to account for his absence.

American comedian Harry Parke, known for his performances as 'Parkyakarkus', a pun on 'park your carcass', died at the Friar's Club Roast of Lucille Ball and Desi Arnaz in Los Angeles, California, on 24 November 1958. The compère, Art Linkletter, had just wrapped up his section with the line, 'How come anyone as funny as this isn't on the air?' when Parke slumped dead onto Milton Berle's lap.

George Reeves, the first Superman on television in the 1950s, committed suicide by shooting himself in 1959.

Baritone Leonard Warren expired on stage after performing his aria in the second act of the opera *La Forza del Destino* at the New York Metropolitan Opera on 4 March 1960.

Nelson Eddy, star of musical films in the 1930s and '40s, was performing at the Sans Souci Hotel in Palm Beach, Florida, in March 1967 when he suffered a cerebral haemorrhage while on stage. He died a few hours later.

Les Harvey, lead guitarist of the Glasgow rock band Stone the Crows, died after being electrocuted by his microphone while performing at Swansea's Top Rank Ballroom on 3 May 1972.

US TV presenter Christine Chubbuck was broadcasting live on her own morning magazine programme, *Suncoast Digest*, in July 1974 when she announced, 'In keeping with Channel 40's policy of bringing you the latest in blood and guts, and in living colour, we bring you another first – an attempted suicide.' She then shot herself in the head with a revolver.

Terry Kath, lead singer of American rock band *Chicago*, died in 1978 while showing off playing 'Russian Roulette' with himself. As he pressed the 9mm pistol to his head, his last words were the same as Johnny Ace's: 'Don't worry, it's not loaded.'

American politician R. Budd Dwyer had been convicted of receiving a bribe but insisted throughout his trial, and after his conviction, that he was innocent and claimed that he had been framed. Matters came to a head, literally, on the morning of 22 January 1987 when he called a television press conference at his office in Harrisburg, Pennsylvania. There he read a statement, advised the press to leave 'if this will offend you', and produced a .357 Magnum revolver: advising people not to come near him, he then opened his mouth wide, inserted the barrel of the gun and pulled the trigger. As a result, TV news editors were left with the quandary of how graphic they wished the footage aired on their channel to be.

Carry On star Sid James collapsed on stage at the Sunderland Empire during a performance of the farce *The Mating Game* on 26 April 1976. The curtains were closed and a doctor was called but the audience laughed, believing the events to be part of the show. Sid was taken to hospital by ambulance, but died about an hour later.

High-wire daredevil Karl Wallenda died when he lost his balance and fell to his death while walking on a wire that was suspended 123ft in the air between two buildings in San Juan, Puerto Rico, on 22 March 1978.

Comedy magician Tommy Cooper suffered a heart attack and collapsed on stage during a performance on the popular LWT variety show *Live from Her Majesty's*. Thousands of viewers at home, and many in the audience, initially thought it was part of the act but sadly, despite attempts to revive Tommy, he was pronounced dead on arrival at Westminster Hospital on 15 April 1984.

Comedian Eric Morecambe collapsed offstage when he suffered a heart attack immediately after a curtain call of his performance at the Roses Theatre in Tewkesbury, Gloucestershire, on 28 May 1984. Removed to Cheltenham General Hospital, he was pronounced dead five and a half hours later.

TOO SOON: SOME PREMATURE DEPARTURES OF POP LEGENDS

INXS lead singer Michael Hutchence (thirty-seven) was found naked and suspended, by his belt, from an automatic door closure at the Ritz-Carlton hotel in Double Bay, Sydney, Australia, in November 1997. His wife, the late Paula Yates, was convinced it had not been an act of suicide but one of auto-erotic asphyxiation.

One legend is that Mama Cass (thirty-two), lead singer with the popular '60s band The Mamas and the Papas, choked to death on a chicken (or ham) sandwich in July 1974. Her post-mortem, however, recorded that no food was found in her windpipe and that she had, in fact, died of a heart attack. But where she died really does have a strange tale to tell. American singer songwriter Harry Nilsson, the singer of the tragic hit 1970s 'Without You', often let musician friends stay at his flat in Curzon Place, Mayfair, London, while he was away. Cass was on tour in the UK and was staying at Nilsson's flat when she died. Four years later, in 1978, Keith Moon, the drummer with The Who, was also staying at the flat, in the very same room as Cass, when he died from an overdose of a prescribed anti-alcohol drug.

Buddy Holly (twenty-two) died when the aircraft carrying him, along with J.P. 'The Big Bopper' Richardson and Ritchie Valens, crashed in Grant Township, Cerro Gordo County, Iowa, USA, on 3 February 1959.

Elvis Presley (forty-six) was found dead from heart failure on his bathroom floor at his magnificent home of Graceland, Memphis, Tennessee, on 16 August 1977.

Folk legend Sandy Denny (thirty-one) died on 21 April 1978 from a brain haemorrhage. It was caused by injuries she sustained after falling down a flight of stairs outside a friend's flat in a house in Hammersmith, London.

Marc Bolan (twenty-nine) died two weeks before his thirtieth birthday on 16 September 1977 when the mini being driven by his girlfriend, soul star Gloria Jones, failed to negotiate a humpback bridge and ploughed into a sycamore tree near Gipsy Lane, Queens Ride, Barnes, London, killing Bolan instantly and injuring Jones. The site soon became a shrine for his fans and was officially recognised as Bolan's Rock Shrine in 2007.

Janice Joplin (twenty-seven) was found dead from a heroin overdose (possibly combined with the effects of alcohol) in her room at the Landmark Hotel, Los Angeles, California, USA, on 4 October 1970.

Sid Vicious (twenty-one), bass player in the legendary punk-rock group The Sex Pistols, died of a heroin overdose after a party at his girlfriend's apartment on Bank Street, New York, on 2 February 1979.

Joy Division lead singer Ian Curtis (twenty-three) committed suicide by hanging himself in the kitchen of his house on 18 May 1980.

Karen Carpenter (thirty-two), one half of the 1970s singing combo The Carpenters, died at her parents' home in Downey, California, on 4 February 1983. The Los Angeles coroner gave the primary cause of death as 'heartbeat irregularities brought on by chemical imbalances associated with anorexia nervosa.'

Rap star Tupac Shakur (twenty-five) died from the wounds he received after being gunned down in a drive-by shooting in Las Vegas, Nevada, on 31 September 1996.

Patsy Cline (thirty) died when the plane she was in hit bad weather and crashed into a forest outside Camden, Tennessee, USA, on 5 March 1963.

Country and easy listening legend 'Gentleman' Jim Reeves (forty) was killed on 31 July 1964 when the plane he was flying was caught in a thunderstorm and crashed into a wooded area north-northeast of Brentwood, approximately at the junction of Baxter Lane and Franklin Pike Circle and southwest of Nashville International Airport, Tennessee, USA, where Reeves had planned to land.

Jim Morrison (twenty-seven), lead singer with The Doors, was found dead in the bath of the apartment he rented with his girlfriend on the Rue Beautreillis, Paris, on 3 July 1971. The medical examiner stated that there was no evidence of foul play and so, pursuant to French law, Morrison was buried without a post-mortem. As a result, the precise cause of his death remains shrouded in mystery.

John Denver (fifty-three) died when the Rutan Long-EZ aircraft he was flying crashed into the Pacific Ocean near Pacific Grover, California, on 12 October 1997.

Jimi Hendrix (twenty-seven) died after asphyxiating on his own vomit at his girlfriend's flat at the Samarkand Hotel on Lansdowne Crescent, Notting Hill, London, on 18 September 1970. Indeed, The Jimi Hendrix Experience, his band, was also the first 'super group' to be claimed by the grim reaper: bassist Noel Redding (fifty-seven) died of cirrhosis of the liver in May 2003, and drummer Mitch Mitchell (sixty-one) died in his sleep of natural causes in November 2008.

THE LAST WORDS OF ADAM FAITH

Adam Faith was one of the biggest names on the pop and entertainment scene in the 1960s. His regular chart hits, such as 'What Do You Want?' and 'Someone Else's Baby', saw him become a teen idol and he then progressed to have further successes in the lead role of the 1970s television series *Budgie*. Faith continued to appear in a variety of roles on television until his death, from a heart attack, in North Staffordshire Hospital on 8 March 2003. His last words, commenting on a bad night of television offerings, were reported in a number of British tabloids, and were as follows: 'Channel Five is all s***, isn't it? Christ, the crap they put on there. It's a waste of space.'

RIP DRACULA

Bela Lugosi, the man who had popularised the role of Dracula on the big screen in the late 1920s and '30s (and synonymous with various reprisals of the role up to the time of his death in 1956), was buried in one of his Dracula costumes, complete with cape.

THE CROW

Brandon Lee, son of martial arts film legend Bruce Lee, died when he received a shot from a prop gun fired by actor Michael Massee's character while filming a scene for *The Crow*. The shot perforated Lee's stomach, tearing several vital organs and causing an internal haemorrhage. He was rushed to the New Hanover Regional Medical Center in Wilmington, NC, where a six-hour operation was attempted to save Brandon's life, but died at 1.03 p.m. on 31 March 1993. The shooting was ruled an accident and no blame attached to Mr Massee, but the poor man was devastated by what had happened. Contrary to urban legend, the footage of his death was not kept in the movie. Instead, they re-shot the scene using a different actor, whose death in the film was caused by a throwing knife.

THE LATE BOB MARLEY

Plans for a BBC documentary about reggae singer Bob Marley in 2005 went awry when researchers approached the Bob Marley Foundation to see if the singer would be prepared to spend a few days with them: indeed, their e-mail emphasised the programme 'would only work with some participation from Bob Marley himself'. The programme makers had apparently failed to realise that the singer had been dead for over twenty years.

NOW GET OUT OF THAT

In October 1990 escape artist Joseph 'Amazing Joe' Burrus was trying to make a name for himself with a major stunt to rival one of Houdini's – an escape from chains and handcuffs inside a clear plastic coffin placed in a 7ft-deep grave, upon which would be piled 3ft of soil, with 6,000lb of wet concrete poured on top of that. Performing the act seemed to be going to plan at Blackbeard's Fun Centre, Fresno, California, but as the concrete was poured in the coffin collapsed under the combined pressure of the materials piled on top and Joe was asphyxiated beneath an estimated 7 tons of soil and earth.

THREE FATAL PERFORMANCES

A Mrs Fitzherbert of Northamptonshire came to London's famous Drury Lane Theatre to see *The Beggar's Opera* in 1782. She found Mr

Bannister's performance of Polly so hilarious that she lost all control and was respectfully requested to leave the theatre. Her hysterics continued, however, without intermission for the following two days, when she finally expired.

In 1923 Joseph Chatfield, aged seventy-nine, went to see a Charlie Chaplin film in a Hammersmith cinema and laughed so hard he died.

Then there was King's Lynn bricklayer Alex Mitchell, aged fifty, who died after roaring with laughter at an episode of BBC comedy series *The Goodies*, starring Graeme Garden, Tim Brooke-Taylor and Bill Oddie, on 24 March 1975.

KILLER SONG

The song 'Gloomy Sunday', composed by Hungarian composer Rezső Seress and published in 1933 as 'Vége a világnak' (End of the World), had a dark reputation. A curse was said to have become attached to the song after Seress's girlfriend, who had ditched him for a wealthy man, killed herself when it was published and became popular. There followed a number of strange incidents; a number of newspapers claimed increasing numbers of suicides – some quoting figures of twenty-five – had been associated with the song. As a result, according to the legend, it was banned by a number of radio stations. Was it fact or urban myth? It is difficult to find evidence for many instances of the song being banned, but it is interesting to note that the BBC banned Billie Holiday's version of the song for 'being detrimental to wartime morale' – the ban was only lifted in 2002. Seress also committed suicide, although some thirty-five years after writing the song. He jumped out of a window in Budapest but survived the fall – so, while in the hospital, he choked himself to death with a wire.

WHEN KNIFE THROWING GOES WRONG...

According to a report published in *The Illustrated Police News* in March 1876, pretty vocalist and danseuse Julia Bernard volunteered to be the assistant for a knife thrower at a show in New York. He managed to complete the majority of his routine, throwing six knives that deftly landed between each arm, just above each shoulder, one either side of her head. The last knife was to end up just above her head, but the knife thrower miscalculated and the blade went flying into her forehead. It penetrated her brain, killing her instantly.

FIRE DANCE

During a grand performance at Day's Crystal Palace Concert Hall in Birmingham in March 1868, as part of the ballet scene, one of the dancers, named Fanny Smith, struck the wick of a lamp on the stage with a wand that she was carrying. A portion of the wick, saturated with flammable liquid, fell upon her dress and promptly set it on fire and in moments she was enveloped in flames. The audience went into a panic and poor Fanny was left rushing on stage and then off until the fire was smothered by a gentleman who rolled her in his coat. Fanny was rushed to the Queen's Hospital, where she died a few days later.

DEATH AND THE MAIDEN

Elizabeth Rossetti, wife of Dante Gabriel Rossetti, poet, painter and one of the founder members of the Pre-Raphaelite Brotherhood, died from an overdose of laudanum in 1862. Overcome with grief for his darling wife, Rossetti buried her with the manuscript and sole copy of the poems he had written to her over the years, nesting it between her cheek and hair. In 1869 Rossetti was persuaded to have her exhumed and the book removed so that the poems could be published. After disinfection and cleaning of the manuscript, the finished volume was published in 1870.

THE MURDER OF 'BREEZY BILL'

William 'Breezy Bill' Terriss, one of the most popular actors of his day, was stabbed to death at his private entrance to the Adelphi Theatre in London by Richard Archer Prince in December 1897. Prince, known to acquaintances as 'Mad Archie', was an inveterate letter writer who sent high-handed missives to theatrical managers who offended him or sent fawning letters of commiseration or congratulations to royalty or celebrities, depending on the occasion. He was thought harmless enough by most. During the run of *The Harbour Lights*, in which Prince had a minor role, Terriss took offence to a comment Prince made about him and had Prince dismissed. Terriss, however, sent small sums of money to Prince, via the Actors' Benevolent Fund, and continued to try to find him acting engagements. In December 1897 Prince attempted to get a complimentary ticket to the vaudeville theatre which adjoined the Adelphi; he was turned down and forcibly ejected. Prince brooded on this event and a combination of jealousy of Terriss's success and anger (for he blamed Terriss for his situation) drove him to murder. Prince stepped out of the shadows the following evening and carried out his revenge. Convicted of the murder but found insane, Prince spent the rest of his years at Broadmoor Criminal Lunatic Asylum, occasionally putting on concerts with the other inmates until his death there in 1936. The ghost of William Terriss is said to haunt both the Adelphi Theatre and Covent Garden tube station.

CHAMPAGNE CHARLIE

One of the most popular songs of late Victorian England was 'Champagne Charlie', a song popularised by George Leybourne, who trod the boards of London music halls; immaculately turned out in tails and top hat and sporting a monocle, he was the archetypal 'tipsy gent'.

The tragedy is that most of the time he was not acting: having squandered all his money on drink, Leybourne died, lonely and penniless, at his Islington home in 1884. He is buried in Abney Park, Stoke Newington, under the epitaph, 'God's finger touched him and he slept.'

THE LAST REVIEW

The epitaph for comedian Thomas Jackson, Gillingham, Norfolk, reads:

> Sacred to the memory of THOMAS JACKSON, Comedian, who was engaged December 21st, 1741, to play a comic cast of characters in this great theatre, the world, for many of which he was prompted by nature to excel – The season being ended – his benefit over – the charges all paid, and his account closed, he made his exit in the tragedy of Death, on the 17th of March, 1798, in full assurance of being called once more to rehearsal, and where he hopes to find his forfeits all cleared, his cast of parts bettered, and his situation made agreeable by Him who paid the great stock debt, for the love He bore to performers in general.

UPRIGHT BEN JONSON

Dramatist, poet and scholar Ben Jonson was being railed by the Dean of Westminster about being buried in Poet's Corner; always mindful of his lack of finances, Jonson replied, 'I am too poor for that and no one will lay out funeral charges upon me. No, Sir, six feet long and two feet wide is too much for me; two feet by two feet will do for all I want.' 'You shall have it,' replied the Dean. Jonson, who died on 6 August 1637, has the unique distinction to be the only body buried standing on his feet in Westminster Abbey.

LAST WORD ON THE BARD

William Shakespeare's funerary monument in Holy Trinity church, Stratford-upon-Avon, reads:

Judicio Pylium, genio Socratem, arte Maronem,
Terra tegit, populus mœret, Olympus habet.

Stay, passenger, why dost thou go so fast?
Read, if thou canst, what envious death hath placed
Within this monument, Shakespeare, with whom
Quick nature died; whose name doth deck the tomb
Far more than cost, sith all that he hath writ
Leaves living art but page unto his wit.

Shakespeare's monument also displays the verse:

Good friend, for Jesu's sake forbeare
To dig the dust enclosed here;
Blessed be he that spares these stones,
And curst be he that moves my bones.

BULLSEYE

A strange story, which may or may not be urban myth, is that the popular TV darts quiz show *Bullseye,* hosted by comedian Jim Bowen between 1982 and 1995, was responsible for saving the lives of hundreds of suicidal men over the years. The danger period when men are most likely to take their own lives is Sunday afternoon and early evening – exactly the time frame when the show was aired. When the show was on, according to the theory, depressed men would be distracted enough to want to see the outcome of each round. By the time the show ended the most dangerous time was over. It was said that the suicide rate in men was noted to rise between each season of the show.

SOME CELEBRITY SUICIDES

George Sanders: Star of classic films including *All About Eve* (1950), *Rebecca* (1940) and *The Jungle Book* (1967) (as the voice of Shere Khan), took an overdose in 1972. He left a note saying, 'Dear World, I am leaving because I am bored. I feel I have lived long enough. I am leaving you with your worries in this sweet cesspool. Good luck.'

Adolf Hitler: Shot himself with James Bond's gun, a Walther PPK. His wife, Eva, took a cyanide pill.

Vincent van Gogh: Shot himself in the chest with a revolver before walking home to die, in bed, after smoking a pipe.

Ernest Hemingway: After an adventurous life that saw him survive two world wars, a mortar strike, a car crash, two plane crashes and a bushfire, he shot himself in the head with his favourite shotgun on 2 July 1961.

Alan Turing: Vilified and chemically castrated after an 'indecency' trial, the 'father of computer science' is thought to have committed suicide by eating an apple coated in cyanide in 1954. Over fifty years later, Prime Minister Gordon Brown officially apologised in 2009 for 'the appalling way he was treated'.

Sylvia Plath: Pulitzer Prize-winning poet who died from carbon monoxide poisoning after putting her head in the oven on 11 February 1963.

Virginia Woolf: Phyllis Rose's *Woman of Letters* includes writer Virginia Woolf's suicide note to her husband: 'Dearest,' she wrote, 'I feel certain that I am going mad again. I feel we can't go through another of those terrible times. And I shan't recover this time. I begin to hear voices, and I can't concentrate. So I am doing what seems the best thing to do. You have given me the greatest possible happiness … I don't think two people could have been happier than we have been. V.' Woolf then put on her overcoat and, after filling the pockets with stones, walked the short distance from her home to the River Ouse and drowned herself.

Kurt Cobain: The Nirvana frontman died from a self-inflicted shotgun blast on 5 April 1994.

SPIKE'S EPITAPH

Comedy legend Spike Milligan always said the epitaph upon his headstone would read, 'I told you I was ill'. When the time came, however, in 2002, Spike was buried at St Thomas's Cemetery, Winchelsea, East Sussex – but the Chichester diocese refused to allow the epitaph. A compromise was found, with the Irish translation, *Dúirt mé leat go raibh mé breoite*, used instead.

10

TERRIBLE TRANSPORT

SOME FIRSTS

The first person to be killed by a railway train was the Right Honourable William Huskisson, who died of his wounds after being run over by George Stephenson's locomotive *The Rocket* at the opening of the Liverpool and Manchester Railway on 15 September 1830.

The first person to be killed by a motor vehicle was Bridget Driscoll of Old Town, Croydon, who was crossing the grounds of the Crystal Palace, on the way to a dancing display, when a Roger-Benz car knocked her down and killed her instantly on the morning of 17 August 1896.

The first driver to die from injuries sustained in a motoring accident was Mr Henry Lindfield of Brighton, who died from shock on Sunday 13 February 1898 following the amputation of his leg as a result of his electrical carriage overturning the previous day.

The first passenger to die as a result of a car accident was Major James Stanley Richer, who was seriously injured during the demonstration drive of a 6HP Daimler Wagonette on 25 February 1899 when the rear wheel collapsed and both men – Richer and his driver – were thrown from the car at Grove Hill, Harrow. The driver was killed on the spot and the Major died four days later. As an aside, the driver, Mr Edwin Sewell, also achieved a first – he became the first driver of a petrol-driven car to die in an accident.

The first person to die in a crash of a powered aeroplane was First Lieutenant Thomas Etholen Selfridge, US Army, who died when the aircraft he was being flown in – by Orville Wright, no less – crashed at Fort Myer, Arlington, Virginia, USA, on 17 September 1908.

A COACHMAN'S END

Noted coachman James William Selby died of exposure in December 1888. Piloting his coach *Old Times* his exploits and speed were renowned. In the year of his death Selby won a bet for covering the 108-mile journey from London to Brighton in seven hours and fifty minutes. His demise was hardly surprising to those who knew him well: he was out in all weathers – rain, wind and snow would not deter this brave coachman. However, there are only so many times you can get so cold that your hat freezes to your head and has to be steamed off!

LAST WORDS ON A COACHMAN

Epitaph for William Salter, driver of the Yarmouth stagecoach, who died in 1776, and whose monument is displayed upon the wall of Haddiscoe church, Norfolk:

Here lies Will Salter, honest man,
Deny it, Envy, if you can;
True to his business and his trust,
Always punctual, always just;
His horses, could they speak, would tell
They loved their good old master well.
His up-hill work is chiefly done,
His stage is ended, race is run;
One journey is remaining still,
To climb up Sion's holy hill.
And now his faults are all forgiven,
Elijah-like, drives up to heaven,
Takes the reward of all his pains,
And leaves to other hands the reins.

OFF-ROAD AND KILLER SHEEP

A farmer's wife went to feed the sheep on the farm in January 1999 riding an off-road quad bike loaded with a bale of hay. Mobbed by the animals, the bike, with the wife still on board, was sent fatally careering over the edge of Ashes Quarry in Stanhope, Durham.

ROBERT KILLED BY ROBOT

The first recorded death of a man caused by a robot occurred at a casting plant in Flack Rock, Michigan, USA, in 1979, when Ford engineer Robert Williams was slammed in the head by a robot arm as he was gathering parts in a storage facility. His family were awarded $10 million in damages.

DRIVE THRU AND DRIVE BY

For maximum comfort and convenience the Robert L. Adams Funeral Parlour in Compton, southern Los Angeles, has offered drive-through viewing of the dearly departed between 6 p.m. and 9 p.m. for the last forty years. And because the glass partition is bullet proof, it remains popular for gangland funerals.

FORTUNES OF WAR

According to statistics published by the Royal Society for the Prevention of Accidents in 1941, over the previous twelve months there had been six cases of pedestrians being killed by bumping into each other; five of these incidents occurred during the blackout. Twenty-two others were killed by walking into lamp-posts or other obstructions or slipping on pavements. Thousands of people died in the blackout during the Second World War, with no help from enemy action. Road accidents increased to unprecedented levels because of the extinguished street lights and masked lights on the vehicles traversing the dark roads. The peak year of road deaths was 1940, when a total of 9,169 people lost their lives through accidents, mostly in the blackout.

ACCIDENT BLACKSPOTS

According to statistics published by the Road Safety Foundation, an average of six people are killed on British roads every day; road crashes have killed 30,000 people in Britain over the last decade and seriously injured 300,000. They name the top ten British accident blackspots as:

1. A537 Macclesfield to Buxton – Cheshire/Derbyshire
2. A5012 Pikehall to Matlock – Derbyshire
3. A621 Baslow to Totley – Derbyshire/South Yorkshire
4. A625 Calver to Sheffield – South Yorkshire
5. A54 Congleton to Buxton – Derbyshire
6. A581 Rufford to Chorley – Lancashire
7. A5004 Whaley Bridge to Buxton – Derbyshire
8. A675 Blackburn to Preston – Lancashire
9. A61 Barnsley to Wakefield – South/West Yorkshire
10. A285 Chichester to Petworth – West Sussex

THE CURSED CAR OF SARAJEVO

The 1911 Gräf & Stift Double Phaeton carrying the Archduke Franz Ferdinand and his wife, Sophie, Duchess of Hohenberg, when they were assassinated on 28 June 1914 – the act that sparked the First World War – was restored to pristine condition by the Governor of Yugoslavia after the end of the war. He ignored any suggestion that the car might be tainted or cursed in any way – though the Governor was persuaded otherwise after four accidents, one of which resulted in the loss of his own right arm. He was determined to have the vehicle destroyed but his friend, Dr Srikis, disagreed, and he too dismissed any notion of a curse. He was found on the road under the overturned vehicle six months later.

The next owner was another doctor, but when his patients began to mysteriously desert him he sold the car on to a Swiss racing driver. While taking part in a road race in the Dolomites, the driver was thrown out of the car and died from a broken neck. The next owner was a farmer who was in the process of towing it in for repairs, assisted by another local farmer, when the car roared back to life and hurtled off at full speed – killing both agriculturalists. The car's last private owner was one Tiber Hirschfield, who thought the curse of the car might be lifted if it was repainted in a more cheerful livery. The brighter car – now blue – was to be the ideal transport for Hirschfield and five friends to drive to a wedding. It proved to be less than ideal, however, as Tiber and four of his guests were killed when the car was involved in a head-on collision on the way.

The cursed car made its final journey when it was shipped to the Heeresgeschichtliches Museum (Museum of Military History) in Vienna, Austria, where it was cared for by Karl Brunner. He would regale visitors with tales of 'the curse' and forbade anyone to sit in it. The museum was bombed during the Second World War: the car was damaged, as was poor Karl Brunner, who would not live to tell his tales again.

SAILING DIE

Approximately 1,000 people have died over the last five years on cruise ships that ran aground or sank. Over three quarters of those deaths occurred in a single disaster, the MV *Princess of the Stars*, which sank in the Philippines during a typhoon in 2008.

EDDYSTONE LEAD

When the lantern of the Eddystone lighthouse caught fire in December 1755, ninety-four-year-old Henry Hall was the keeper of the watch. He did his best to put out the fire by throwing water upwards from a bucket. However, while doing so the leaden roof melted and – horrifically – the molten lead ran down over him, burning him badly; his mouth was open whilst looking up and some of the molten lead ran down his throat. He continued to try to fight the fire but all was lost. Henry died twelve days later. Doctor Spry of Plymouth, who had attended Hall as he died, performed a post-mortem and found a flat oval piece of lead in his stomach that weighed 7oz. Dr Spry wrote an account of his findings in this case to the Royal Society of Fellows but the Society were very sceptical. Spry was not happy to be doubted and for the sake of his reputation he carried out experiments on dogs and fowls and proved that they could live after having molten lead poured down their throats. In case you doubt me, the piece of lead from Hall's stomach may be seen in the Edinburgh Museum.

THE PRINCESS ALICE DISASTER

The *Princess Alice* was one of the most popular pleasure steamers on the Thames – so popular, in fact, that returning from Sheerness on the evening of 3 September 1878 she was overloaded by about 200 passengers. Her official capacity was 500 passengers. As *Princess Alice* entered the stretch near Barking Creek, the ironclad collier *Bywell Castle* (a vessel five times the weight of the *Princess Alice*) loomed ahead; it was en route to Newcastle to take coals on for Alexandria. For some reason Captain Grinstead of the *Princess Alice* suddenly changed course and the *Bywell Castle* could not manoeuvre away in time: emerging out of the darkness and ploughing its bows just forward of the starboard paddle box, the collision almost cut the *Princess Alice* in two. The cruiser sank in less than four minutes. More than 640 people drowned, and many of the bodies were never recovered. The Thameside towns of Rainham, East Ham and Barking were deeply affected by the disaster and a subscription was raised for the bereaved. In the days afterwards the waters around Woolwich were filled with any small vessel the enterprising could get their hands on – recovered bodies earned their finder 12s a carcass, and many unseemly struggles and fights to recover the dead ensued.

11

A DEADLY GAME
OF SPORTS

'INVINCIBLE' HARRIS

The first British professional cyclist to be killed in a cycling race was Bert 'Invincible' Harris. During his last, fatal race, held at Aston on Easter Monday 1897, his cycle touched another vehicle and he was upset, head-first, onto the track. Removed to the Birmingham General Hospital, Harris died of his injuries a few days later, on 21 April 1897, never having regained consciousness. He was twenty-four years old. Tens of thousands of mourners lined the streets of Leicester for his funeral procession. The memorial erected to him at Welford Road Cemetery in the town states:

This memorial stone is erected by the cyclists of England in token of the sincere respect and esteem in which he was held by wheelmen the world over.

He was ever a fair and honourable rider and sportsman and his lamented death cut off in its prime one of the brightest and most genial spirits of cycledom.

THE BOXER

Memorial to Alexander 'Sandy' M'Kay, a Scottish giant, who was killed in a bare-knuckle prize fight with Simon Byrne:

Sacred to the memory of

ALEX. M'KAY,
(Late of Glasgow),
Who died 3rd June, 1834,
Aged 26 years.
Strong and athletic was my frame;
Far from my native home I came,
And manly fought with Simon Byrne;
Alas! But lived not to return.
Reader, take warning of my fate.
Lest you should rue your case too late:
If you ever have fought before,
Determine now to fight no more.

HOLE IN ONE

Seventy-nine-year-old Emil Kijek of North Atteboro, Massachusetts, achieved his first ever hole-in-one while golfing at the Sun Valley Golf Course in Rehoboth in December 1994. The excitement of the achievement was clearly too much for him, for as he approached the ball, he simply said 'Oh no', collapsed and died.

KEEP YOUR HEAD

Welsh racing driver J.G. Parry-Thomas was killed at Pendine Sands on the shores of Camarthen Bay on the south coast of Wales in March 1937 while trying to regain his own land-speed record. As his car reached 170mph, the right-hand drive chain snapped. Unfortunately, Parry-Thomas always drove with his head out to the right of the open-topped racing car, and he received the full force of the chain. He suffered fatal head injuries.

THE DOOM OF THE PE TEACHER

PE teacher Jon Desborough was attempting to retrieve a thrown javelin during one of his lessons at Liverpool College in 1999 when he unfortunately lost his footing, tripped and fell onto the blunt end – which passed through his eye socket and penetrated his brain. The injury inflicted massive brain damage, leaving Desborough in a coma; he died a month later.

BIRD STRIKE

Alan Stacey was killed while driving in his Lotus 18 Climax during the 1960 Belgian Grand Prix, at Spa Francorchamps, when he crashed at 120mph after being hit in the face by a bird.

BAD SERVICE

American tennis linesman Richard 'Dick' Wertheim died at the 1983 US Open Tennis Tournament after receiving an errant serve directly into his groin from Stefan Edberg. The blow caused Dick to fall: he hit his head on a pavement and died from blunt cranial trauma.

TEMPER

In 1994 sixteen-year-old Jeremy Brenno of Gloversville, New York, was so angry about his bad shot during a game of golf that he gave his 3 wood a good whack against a bench. The shaft broke, his club bounced back, and the broken piece pierced his pulmonary vein, killing him almost instantly.

DEATH AT THE BOAT RACES

A fatal accident occurred at Cambridge Boat Races in 1888 after the Clare College boat bumped Queen's at First Post Corner;

Queen's were drawing to the bank. The Trinity Hall boat then came up, hotly pursued by Emmanuel, who had made their bump. The Trinity boat ran over the iron riggers into the Clare boat, and the prow of it penetrated the chest of Mr E.S. Campbell of the Clare College crew, literally lifting him from his seat. He received the blow over the region of the heart, between two ribs, and died within a few minutes.

THE OLYMPIAN

Stella Walsh, winner of forty-one American championships, of the gold medal for the 100m at the 1932 Los Angeles Olympics and of the silver in Berlin in 1936, was tragically killed by a stray bullet during a robbery in 1980. Her autopsy revealed she possessed male genitalia.

THE LONG WALK TO THE PAVILLION

Mr E.R. Carr, twenty-nine, captain of the Albemarle Cricket Club, was playing away at the Leyton ground and scored a respectable twenty-nine runs before he was caught out in August 1882. As he was retiring to the tent the crowd cheered him for his batting – to the degree that it 'excited him and he fell down in a fainting fit'. His colleagues gathered around him, and restoratives were administered, but he never regained consciousness. He died a short while later.

STRIKE!

Don Doane had been a member of the same Michigan ten-pin-bowling team for forty-five years when he finally managed to rack up his first perfect score of the maximum 300 in 2008. As he was high fiving his teammates in celebration the excitement proved too much for him, and he collapsed and died of a heart attack.

SHOT BY A FISH

According to a report published in *Pearson's Weekly*, in 1931 a Canadian fisherman was shot and killed by a fish. After catching the 'fine' creature, the fisherman dropped it into the bottom of his canoe, where it got tangled in his fishing line. The line fouled itself around the trigger of his loaded rifle and discharged the weapon at the hunter at point-blank range.

NOT LBW

The great Norfolk and Kent cricketer William Pilch died of 'mortification of the big toe' on 4 September 1866.

THE CRICKETER'S EPITAPH

I bowled, I struck, I caught, I stopt,
Sure life's a game of cricket;
I block'd with care, with caution popp'd,
Yet Death has hit my wicket.

RUNNING MAN

Daniel Cox was an athletic young man competing in a foot race staged at Sedgley, West Midlands, in May 1883. As the competitors entered Wombourne Road, Cox stumbled and fell against a wall with such violence that he broke his neck and died on the spot.

DEATH AT THE RACES

The only deceased jockey ever to win a steeplechase was American Frank Hayes, who rode 20-1 outsider Swiss Key to victory at Belmont Park in New York in 1923. When the horse's owner and trainer went over to congratulate him immediately after the race he simply slumped forward. He was quite dead. A subsequent medical examination revealed he had died of a fatal heart attack during the race and had been dead when he romped across the finish line.

THE REF STRIKES BACK

According to Reuters, in July 2004 a South African soccer referee pulled a gun and shot dead a coach who questioned one of his rulings. Inspector Mali Govender of the Grahamstown Police in the Eastern Cape Province said a fight broke out after the referee gave a yellow warning card to a player in a local match: 'there was an altercation and the referee became threatened when the other team approached him because they were angry,' Govender said. 'So he pulled out a gun and killed the coach of the visiting team.' The coach died on the field and the referee fled the scene, but Inspector Mali was keen to add that they were confident of making an arrest in the near future.

12

PORTENDS
OF DEATH

British folklore is full of death portents. For example:

Fires and candles, it is said, can warn of a forthcoming death. A candle can predict a winding sheet for a corpse if, after it has gathered, a strip of wax or tallow, instead of being absorbed into the general tallow, remains upright and not melted by the flame, and is noted to curl away from it; it is a presage of death to the person in whose direction it points.

If a hollow oblong cinder is spat out of the fire it is a sign of a death coming to the family.

If the church clock strikes the hour while the congregation is singing on Sunday there will be a death in the parish the next week.

If a grave is left open on a Sunday, there will be another dug before the week is out.

If the church clock 'loses a stroke' or refuses to go properly a death will be known in the village.

It is considered unlucky for anyone, other than the proper officials, to toll the death bell. The stranger is said to ring his own death bell.

If the body of the deceased remains supple after death it is a sign that another death will take place in the family within the year.

Churches would once be scrupulously cleaned by Candlemas Day (2 February) every year, for it was believed if any remnant of Christmas garland, be it leaf or berry, was left in a family pew, a death would occur in that family before the year was out. It was even known for village gentry to send a servant to check family pews were free of 'danger' on Candlemas Eve.

During the interval between death and burial a body is spoken of as 'lying by the wall'. An old saying states: 'If one lie by the wall on Sunday there will be another [another corpse in the same parish] before the week is out.'

In many rural agricultural areas it was believed if a seed drill went from one end of a field to another without depositing a seed (an accident that may occur as a result of the tubes or coulters clogging with earth), some person connected with the farm would die before the year was out.

The howling of a dog at night in front of your house, particularly near a room where there is a sick-bed, betokens a death.

If the cuckoo gives his note from a dead tree it bodes a coming death to a relative.

The screech of an owl flying past the window of a sick-room signifies death is near.

If a corpse is carried along any path, it (the path) can never be done away with.

Tablecloths and particularly sheets should be carefully examined for oval creases known as 'coffin folds', thought to signify imminent illness or a fatality to the household.

If it be 'lowering' or wet on Childermas or Innocent's Day (28 December), it threatens scarcity and mortality among the weaker sort of young people.

A tradition recorded in Worcestershire said that storm, rains or other 'elemental strifes' will take place at the moment of death of a great man and that the 'spirit of the storm' will not be appeased until the moment of burial.

Three raps on a bed's head is an unwelcome greeting as it warns of death.

To hear the cuckoo's first note in bed forebodes illness or death to the hearer or one of their family.

The breaking of a wedding ring is regarded as a sign that the wearer will soon be a widow.

Taking a sprig of blackthorn, when in blossom, into a house is thought to presage death to a member of the family.

If you overturn a loaf of bread in the oven, you will have a death in the house.

If a swarm of bees alight either on a dead tree or dead bough of a living tree near the house, there will be a death in the family in the near future.

The tradition of 'telling the bees' of a death in the family was once a well-observed custom, for it was believed the bees would take such offence they would desert their hives if they were not informed. A procession would be formed up to make the formal announcement to the bees and sundry pieces of black cloth, and the key to the main door of the house, were taken to the hives. A piece of black cloth was then solemnly bound around each hive, given three taps with the key and the bees informed their master was dead.

Watch the porch of the parish church on St Mark's Eve – the apparitions of those who will die will walk in and stay in; those who will be seriously ill but will recover will drift in, linger and float out again. (It was said sextons observed this to count the gains for the coming year.)

DIVINING A DROWNED BODY

Wednesday, 8 April 1767: 'An inquisition was taken at Newbury, Berkshire, on the body of a child near two years old, who fell into the river Kennet, and was drowned. The jury brought a verdict of accidental death. The body was discovered by a very singular experiment, which was as follows:- After diligent search had been made in the river for the child, to no purpose, a two-penny loaf, with a quantity of quicksilver put into it, was set floating from the place where the child, it was supposed, had fallen in, which steered its course down the river upwards of half a mile, before a great number of spectators, when the body happening to lay on the contrary side of the river, the loaf suddenly tacked about, and swam across the river and gradually sank near the child.' (*Gentleman's Magazine*, vol. 37)

HAIL TO THE CHIEF

One curious tale tells of the curse of Native American Tecumseh, a chieftain of the Shawneee tribe, who cursed 'the great white fathers' after suffering defeat at the Battle of Tippecanoe at the hands of William Henry Harrison in 1811. Tecumseh died in the Battle of the Thames in 1813 – again, at the hands of Harrison. The curse, it is claimed, damned every US President elected in years evenly divisible by twenty. So far it is said to have claimed the lives of Presidents:

> William Henry Harrison (1840)
> Abraham Lincoln (1860)
> James A. Garfield (1880)
> William McKinley (1900)
> Warren G. Harding (1920)
> Franklin D. Roosevelt (1940)
> John F. Kennedy (1960)

It is argued the curse was broken in 1981 after Ronald Reagan (elected 1980) survived an assassination attempt.

CULLED AT SIXTY

A letter was received by the Chief Inspector of Margate Police headed 'Corbett Smith on his self-dispatch', from a former BBC executive, Major Arthur Corbett-Smith, in 1945. Read out at the inquest into his death, the letter explained it was Corbett-Smith's firm belief that all sixty-year-old people whose 'continued existence does not in some measure benefit the community' should be humanely killed in a 'lethal chamber'. He certainly acted upon his own advice: having attained the age of sixty he found a spot on Margate Promenade, covered his head with a Union Flag, pressed a revolver to his head, pulled the trigger and blew out his brains.

13

DEATH RITES

STAKED AT THE CROSSROADS

Until the 1850s, people who committed suicide were very rarely buried in consecrated ground. If they were fortunate they might just be buried in a distant area in the north of the churchyard where the body would be laid, face-down, facing west. Many believed the restless spirits of those who took their own lives would 'walk' to harass those they left behind, so the corpses of suicides would be buried away from the town or village at a four-way crossroads so the ghost would not know which path to take to return. To ensure the body and ghost stayed down it would be 'pinned' with an oaken stake through the heart (a practice

prohibited by Act of Parliament in 1823). Crowds would gather around the local sexton as he performed this duty at the wayside grave; even children would risk the wrath of their parents by creeping along and looking through the legs of those assembled at the grim rite.

THE MECCA OF SUICIDES

More suicides have occured at Cleopatra's Needle than at any other site in London. Many have suggested this is because of a curse first brought about by vengeful spirits angered at the removal of the monument from its rightful home in Egypt. An accident even occurred when the 'Needle' was being towed in its special container: the incident occurred during a storm in the Bay of Biscay; the tow ropes had to be cut, and six men drowned. Recovered and towed into Ferrol Harbour, the Needle was eventually brought to England and erected on London's Embankment in 1878.

BURIAL ON THE NORTH SIDE OF THE CHURCHYARD

Burial within, or without, the sanctuary was an important consideration for all burials. In most churchyards the preference is to be buried in the south or east: few wanted to be buried in the shady west, or especially the north. This parcel of land was often believed to be unconsecrated; the superstitious held that the Devil would ride from the north on the Day of Judgement and the souls of suicides and undesirables would form some 'occult wall of protection' for the souls of the righteous elsewhere in the churchyard. In many graveyards a row of graves was placed on the extreme verge. These were the last resting places of the bodies of strangers buried at the parish charge, or of others 'considered unfit to associate underground with the good people of the parish'. The Revd Cullum of Hawstead in Suffolk found this practice 'a vulgar superstition' and voiced his contempt of it in his history of the parish – and in his will, in which he insisted that he be buried at the north door of his church.

A TOKEN OF THANKS

A unique burial custom was observed until the early eighteenth century in the Soken villages of Essex. The gesture of gratitude to the clergyman who read the burial service over the corpse was to offer him (or he had the right to claim) 'the best upper garment' of the dearly departed.

SNUFF ON A CORPSE

An old Irish custom was to place a plate of snuff on the body of the deceased. The etiquette was for all those invited to the funeral to take a pinch on arrival at the laying-in house on the morning of the burial. Hence the Irish retort, 'I'll take a pinch of snuff off your belly yet!'

DEPARTURE OF THE SOUL

In many places doors and windows are opened for a departing soul, but in Exeter they went one step further: it was customary for every locked door, box or cupboard in the house to be unfastened to ease the departure of the soul. In some parts of Britain and on the Continent it was customary to shade the body of a dead child with curtains, away from its parents' gazes, as the soul was supposed to linger in the body as long as a compassionate eye was cast upon it.

SHOULD HE AWAKE

After his death in 1727, Francis Bancroft, London Magistrate and founder of the Mile End Almshouses, left a codicil and bequest in his will that a loaf of bread and a bottle of wine might be placed in his tomb at St Helen's Bishopgate every year on the anniversary of his death, because he was convinced 'that before that time he should awake from his death sleep and require it'.

CAPTAIN BACKHOUSE'S TOMB

About a mile from Great Missenden in Buckinghamshire stands a sort of dwarf pyramid, which is locally called 'Captain Backhouse's tomb'. It is built of flints, strengthened with bricks, and is about 11ft square at the base. The walls, up to about 4-5ft, are perpendicular. After that they taper pyramidically – but, instead of terminating in a point, a flat slab-stone about 3ft square forms the summit. This singular tomb stands in pine wood on an estate once owned by the eccentric Captain Thomas Backhouse.

As he advanced in life his eccentricity increased, and one of his eccentric acts was the erection of his own sepulchre within his own grounds, and under his own superintendence. 'I'll have nothing to do,' said he, 'with the church or the churchyard! Bury me there, in my own wood on the hill, and my sword with me, and I'll defy all the evil spirits in existence to injure me!' He died, at the age of eighty, on 21 June 1800, and was buried, or rather deposited, according to his own directions, in the queer sepulchre he himself had erected. His sword was placed in the coffin with him, and the coffin reared upright within a niche or recess in the western wall, which was then built up in front, so that he was in fact immured.

It is said in the village that he was never married, but had two or three illegitimate sons, one of whom became a Lieutenant-General. This gentleman, returning from India about seven years after his father's death, had Backhouse's body removed to the parish churchyard, placing over his grave a large handsome slab with a suitable inscription. The parish register records:

> August 8th, 1807. The remains of Thomas Backhouse, Esq., removed … from the mausoleum in Havenfield to the churchyard of Great Missenden, and there interred.

IN THE GARDEN

Mr Booth, of Brush House, Yorkshire, desired to be buried in his shrubbery, because he himself had planted it, and passed some of his happiest hours nearby.

Doctor Renny, a physician at Newport Pagnel, Buckinghamshire, was for a similar reason buried in his garden, on a raised plot of ground, surrounded by a sunk fence. In the same county, near a village named Radnage, Thomas Withers, an opulent German, who died on 1 January 1843, at the age of sixty-three, was by his own direction buried 'beneath the shade of his own trees, and in his own ground.'

IN AN OAK TREE

Howel Selyf (or Sele), 7th Lord of Nannau, was reputedly killed by his cousin, Owen Glendower, who then hid his body in a hollow oak tree in the grounds of Nannau, Wales, in 1402. Forty years later a skeleton was found in just such an oak. The tree remained until 1813, when it fell on a still July night soon after being sketched by the antiquary Sir Richard Colt Hoare, who said it then measured 27ft in girth.

OLD SCARLETT,
THE PETERBOROUGH SEXTON

The long-serving sextons of old are often immortalised in the wording on their memorial stones and often on vellum parchment or on a stone tablet in the church. In Peterborough Cathedral there is even a portrait of its long-serving sexton, Robert Scarlett, who died on 2 July 1591 at the age of ninety-eight, 'having buried two generations of his fellow-creatures'. The *Book of Days* (1869) states: 'Two queens had passed through his hands into that bed which gives a lasting rest to queens and to peasants alike. An officer of Death, who had so long defied his principal, could not but have made some impression on the minds of bishop, dean, prebends, and other magnates of the cathedral.' The following lines appear beneath his portrait in the cathedral:

> You see Old Scarlett's picture stand on hie;
> But at your feet here doth his body lye.
> His gravestone doth his age and death-time shew,
> His office by heis token [s] you may know.
> Second to none for strength and sturdy lymm,
> A scare-babe mighty voice, with visage grim;
> He had inter'd two queenes within this place,
> And this townes householders in his life's space
> Twice over; but at length his own time came
> What he for others did, for him the same
> Was done: no doubt his soule doth live for aye,
> In heaven, though his body clad in clay.

A FEMALE SEXTON

Esther Hamilton (1711-1746) was a rare example of a female sexton in the eighteenth century. She followed her father into office at Kingston upon Thames. On one occasion, in 1731, she was digging a grave when the ruins of the church fell down; she lay covered in them for seven hours. Two others were killed, but Esther survived, though she sustained such injury that she was prevented from wearing stays and wore men's garments for the rest of her life.

A CAUTIONARY TALE FOR SEXTONS

John Ricketts was parish sexton at Newington in Surrey. He was solemnly standing by his handiwork as the pall-bearers and coffin were entering the church in October 1804. Suddenly the grave collapsed, and Ricketts was buried to a depth of 6ft. Horrified mourners ran over and tried to dig him out. As more and more onlookers came to see, however, more and more earth fell in. It took over an hour to recover Rickett's lifeless body from its premature grave.

LAST WORDS ON THE SEXTON

William Darnborough, sexton at Hartwith Chapel, Nidderdale, Yorkshire Dales, died on 3 October 1846. His epitaph states:

The graves around for many a year
Were dug by him who slumbers here, —
Till worn with age, he dropped his spade,
And in the dust his bones were laid.

As he now, mouldering, shares the doom
Of those he buried in the tomb;
So shall he, too, with them arise,
To share the judgment of the skies.

PREMATURE BURIAL ALERT

In 1903 Emily Josephine Jepson of Union Lane, Cambridge, obtained
a patent for an unusual invention:

> Improved Coffin for Indicating Burial Alive of a Person in a Trance
> or suffering from a comatose state so that same may be released or
> rescued, has means for admitting air to the coffin and for giving
> audible signal by means of an electric bell, which may be placed
> either on the grave or in the cemetery house. There is a glass plate
> in the lid, and a small shelf attached to one side of the coffin which
> may hold a hammer, matches and candle so that, when the person
> wakes, he can light the candle and with the hammer break the glass
> plate, thus assisting to liberate himself when the earth above the
> coffin is removed.

REST IN PEACE?

Sir Thomas Browne, the notable Norwich physician and philosopher,
was not allowed to rest in peace after his death in October 1682:
his grave was discovered while preparing another in the sanctuary
of St Peter Mancroft church in Norwich in 1840. After a brief
examination, most of his bones were reburied – with the exception of
his skull, hair and coffin plate, which were removed by local chemist
Robert Fitch. Later presented by a Dr Lubbock to the Norfolk and
Norwich Hospital, the relics were displayed in their museum for
many years afterwards. Eventually, in 1922, after an undignified
squabble about its cost and value, the skull was finally reinterred in
a specially made casket with full burial rites. These were especially
tailored to mention the skull's advanced age of 317 years old!

RESTING IN THE RAFTERS

Hertfordshire grocer Henry Trigg was so concerned about having his remains stolen by body-snatchers that he stipulated the beneficiary of his wealth should lay his body to rest in a coffin within the purlins (rafters) of his barn. After Henry's death in 1724, his brother, the Revd Thomas Trigg, put aside any scruples he may have had and ensured Henry's last wishes were fulfilled. There the coffin remained. However, it may well be that Henry's remains did not remain intact after all, as some of the soldiers stationed in the area during the First World War are thought to have plundered his coffin for souvenirs... The coffin, and whatever is left of Henry Trigg within it, is still *in situ* high among the rafters of a building now owned by the Natwest Bank at No. 37 High Street, Old Stevenage.

THE SHEPHERD'S GRAVE

The grave of long-serving shepherd Mr Faithful may be found in a lonely spot on the Chiltern Hills. His epitaph was scoured nearby:

Faithful lived, and Faithful died,
Faithful lies buried on the hill side:
The hill so wide the fields surround,
In the Day of Judgment he'll be found.

In 1861 it was recorded in *Chamber's Book of Days*: 'Up to a recent period the shepherds and rustics of the neighbourhood were accustomed "to scour" the letters: and as they were very large, and the soil chalky, the words were visible at a great distance. The "scouring" having been discontinued, the word "Faithful" alone could be discerned in 1848, but the grave is still held in reverence, and generally approached with solemnity by the rustics of the neighbourhood.'

BASKERVILLE'S FATE

When Birmingham printer John Baskerville, creator of the Baskerville printing font, died, in 1775, he was buried in a tomb of masonry in the shape of a cone under a windmill in the garden of his handsome house.

PLOUGHED

Thomas Hollis was a wealthy landowner who resided on his estate at Corscombe, Dorset. He was eccentric in his habits and remained so in the directions of his will, in which he directed that he should be buried 10ft under the surface in one of his fields, which should then be ploughed over so that no trace of his grave should remain. Curiously, shortly after making his will Hollis was in one of his fields, directing his workman, when he was taken ill. He expired on New Year's Day 1774, aged fifty-four. He was buried according to his wishes.

BEAT THIS

According to chronicler Piccolomini, Czech General Jan Žižka's dying wish in 1424 was to have his skin used to make drums so that he might continue to lead his troops even after death.

SIGN HERE AND WE ASSURE YOU THAT YOU ARE DEAD

In 1896 Arthur Lovell, an opportunist quack doctor, established The London Society for the Prevention of Premature Burial. The service offered a meticulous inspection of the body by their 'specially trained doctors' before funeral procedures were instigated. Those who signed up with the scheme were assured their wishes would be complied with: if the next-of-kin failed to notify the society, or to comply with the stringent terms laid out in the binding contract, the entire estate of the deceased was forfeited to the society.

A TASTE OF DEATH

The effigy figures of three carved wooden crusader knights dating from the 1300s recline in eternal slumber in Danbury church in Essex, but it is one of the nearby floor tombs, thought to be that of Sir Gerard de Braybrooke, who died in March 1422, which now only bears the indentation of the Cross fleury brass which once adorned it, to which one of the most curious stories of the church relates. In October 1779 a grave was being dug in the north aisle for a member of the Ffytche family when a lead coffin was discovered under the old slab. A group of interested gentlemen from Danbury were gathered and the lid was removed, revealing a further resinous shell. This lid was removed to reveal a man of about 5ft dressed in a linen shirt with a narrow 'rude' lace at the neck. The body appeared to be in a perfect condition of preservation, to the degree that when touched the jaws of his mouth opened to the touch and revealed 'a set of perfectly white teeth'. It appeared the preservation was due to the substance in which the knight had been immersed, best described as a 'pickle of sorts' that resembled 'mushroom catsup'. Mr White, the local surgeon, suffering from the lack of a sense of smell, decided to taste the liquid instead. He concluded that it tasted of 'the pickle of Spanish olives'.

WHAT A SEND-OFF

When Sir John Paston died in London in 1466 he was returned to his home county of Norfolk and interred at Bromholm Priory. In the roll of expenses for this grand event, among the lavish preparations, was a note that one man was engaged for three continuous days to flay the beasts for the feast, viz: forty-one pigs, forty-nine calves and ten oxen. With the meat were 1,300 eggs, 20 gallons of milk, and 8 of cream. Fifteen combs of malt were brewed for the occasion; thirteen barrels of beer were provided, twenty-seven of ale and a 'runlet of red wine of 15 gallons'. There was even a barber who was occupied for five days before the event smartening up the monks for the ceremony. The funeral cortège of carriages, carts and entourage was said to have been so long its tail was still been passing through the town of North Walsham (about 4 miles away) when the front wagons entered the priory gates; the 'reke of the torches at the dirge' was so intense a glazier was brought in to remove two window panes to allow the fumes to escape.

THE SPECIFIC DEMANDS OF SIR GILBERT EAST

Sir Gilbert East, who died in 1828, left very specific and quite peculiar directions in his will. His next-of-kin were to see he was buried in the family vault beneath St Nicholas' church at Witham in Essex. They were to order a cedar-wood coffin lined with Russian leather, and see it half-filled with camphor and spices. Sir Gilbert was to then be placed in this prepared coffin and the whole sealed up and put in a wrought-iron coffin painted with six layers of black paint and 'embellished with armorial and funereal devices richly'. This magnificent container was then to be laid next to the body of his wife, and the two encircled with a brass band inscribed, 'Whom God has joined together, let no man put asunder'. The elaborate funeral ceremonies and feasting were to be spread over almost a week – but there was a problem. He had specifically requested to be 'buried in woollen'. This crucial request had been omitted, so poor Sir Gilbert had to be disinterred, re-dressed according to his wishes and interred once again.

IN THE SUMMER HOUSE

The Revd Langdon-Freeman, for many years rector of Bilton, Warwickshire, died on 9 October 1784. He left specific directions in his will: that he should be buried, after lying for four days on the bed upon which he should die, in the summer house of Whilton, where he lived. He desired to be wrapped in a strong winding sheet and 'in all other respects to be interred as near as may be, to the description we receive in Holy Scripture of our Saviour's burial.'

The doors and windows were to be locked or bolted, evergreens planted around the sepulchre and the whole fenced off with iron or oak pales painted in a dark blue colour. His instructions were carried out to the letter. Many years later, in 1860, the old summer house fell into a ruinous state. The building was entered – and there was the reverend, not gone to dust but more like a mummy, or more accurately 'a desiccated cadaver'.

UPSIDE DOWN

When Major Peter Labilliere (spelt Labelliere on his gravestone) died, at the age of seventy-five, in 1800, his final request was that he be buried upside down in a plantation at Box Hill, Dorking, Surrey. This was because he believed the world was a topsy-turvy place and would turn upside down one day – and when that happened he should be righted. Another more prosaic account states that he wished to be buried in that manner in emulation of St Peter.

RESTING IN PEACE OF MIND

In 1896 John Wilmer of Stoke Newington was so concerned about premature burial that he arranged to have his remains interred in the garden of his house. In his hand was a switch, attached to a cable; the cable led to an alarm bell in the house. In case of a system failure, he even stipulated that an examination of the equipment should be carried out annually.

SPONTANEOUS CREMATION

A weird event happened at a funeral in Baton Rouge, Louisiana, in June 1994. Just minutes after the funeral service for a twenty-five-year-old man ended, his body caught fire inside the closed coffin, causing smoke to come shooting out of the cracks. Investigators stated that the only thing that could have caused the dramatic event was embalming fluids spontaneously combusting.

A BIG PROBLEM FOR THE UNDERTAKER

Edward Bright of Maldon was a big man. By the time he was eleven he weighted 10 stone. When he was twelve he was apprenticed to learn the art of the grocer. This may not have been the wisest career choice for a young man who liked his food... Within ten years he was running his own grocer's and tallow chandler's shop, still eating massive meals, and had acquired a taste for mature ales. He also drank about a pint of wine a day. At twenty-two he weighed 30 stone, and by the age of twenty-eight he tipped the scales at 41 stone.

Now morbidly obese, Bright began to suffer with shortness of breath, inflammation of the legs and fever. Each time he fell ill his doctor would bleed him of two pints of blood – after which he was usually 'much restored'. He contracted typhus in late October 1750 and died, in his bed, on 10 November that same year. At the time of his demise, Bright measured 6ft 11in around the belly, 2ft 8in round the middle of his legs and 2ft 2in round the middle of his arms – but stood just 5ft 9in tall. Once the undertaker and his assistants had got his gargantuan body into the coffin there was no way to get it down the stairs: a hole had to be cut through the wall and staircase. When it came to his interment, into a vault near the tower of All Saints' church, a specially built heavy-duty triangle and pulley system was employed.

Then there was Mr Lambert...

Daniel Lambert, one of the biggest men of his age, died suddenly while lodging at the Wagon and Horses Inn in St Martins, Stamford, Lincolnshire, on 21 June 1809. He was just thirty-nine. At the time of his demise Lambert was 5ft 11in tall; his waist was 9ft 4in, his calf measured 3ft 1in at its widest point, and he weighed a massive 52 stone 11lb. His body was taken out of the ground-floor apartments in which he had been accommodated (he had been long incapable of ascending a staircase) by removing the window and part of the wall of the room in which he died to make a passage for the coffin.

Lambert's coffin contained 112ft of elm, and was 6ft 4in long, 4ft 4in wide, and 2ft 4in deep; and the immense substance of his legs necessitated it to be made in the form of a square case. It was built upon two axle-trees, and four cog-wheels, and upon these the remains of the great man were rolled into his grave in the new burial ground of St Martin's churchyard, Stamford. A regular descent was made to the grave by cutting away the earth for some distance. A vast multitude followed the remains to the grave. The most perfect decorum was preserved and not the slightest accident occurred. A headstone and foot stone were later erected there by Daniel's friends back in Leicester.

WILLIAM CAMPBELL THE SCOTTISH GIANT

THE END OF THE SCOTTISH GIANT

William Campbell, the 'giant' landlord of the Duke of Wellington public house in Newcastle-Upon-Tyne, died in 1878. His coffin was 7ft long, 3ft 6in wide and 2ft 10in deep. It was made of elm and lined with lead. There was no way the coffin would fit up the stairs of the pub – and it was only with considerable difficulty and labour that a block and tackle was assembled. It was lifted up three storeys to the outside of the window where the body lay. The window had to be removed entirely, and some of the masonry removed, to enable the coffin to be brought into the room. The body within it was then carefully lowered, but once on the ground no hearse in the town was big enough to take the coffin. A trolley was therefore used to move the coffin – which now weighed about a ton – onto a tradesman's wagon covered in black drapery. The funeral service was well attended: thousands lined the route to watch the spectacle as it passed, and at last Big Willie Campbell was laid to rest in Jesmond Cemetery.

TOM THUMB'S TRAGEDY

Charles Sherwood Stratton, better known as Tom Thumb, part of P.T. Barnum's 'greatest show on earth', stood just 2ft 9in tall; his wife, Lavinia, stood 32in tall. On 5 December 1863 it was revealed that the couple had been blessed with a daughter, named Minnie (after Lavinia's sister), and they embarked on a new tour with babe and entourage which took them back to Britain. While staying in Norwich, however, tragedy struck: young Minnie died, after a short illness, on 25 September 1866. The following day her funeral, at Norwich Cemetery, Earlham, was attended by hundreds of mourners. The route of the glass-sided, horse-drawn hearse was lined by locals curious to see the tiny coffin atop 'a heap of garlands, wreaths and posies'. The chief mourners were simply recorded as 'Mr and Mrs Stratton'.

In later life (after the death of Charles), Lavinia remarried and claimed the baby that they displayed with them was only part of the show and had been borrowed from a home for abandoned children. When the child grew too large it would be taken back and exchanged for a smaller one – in fact, Lavinia was known to claim that Barnum had obtained the babies, for the duration of each tour, from children's homes in the country they were touring, a system she explained as 'English babies in England, French babies in France and German babies in Germany.'

THE BIRMINGHAM MIDGET

Lily Evans died in August 1884, at the age of six weeks and four days. She was less than 13in long, and had become known as 'The Birmingham Midget'. After her death, her mother was anxious to sell the body to a showman. In order to prevent this, deputy coroner Mr Weekes ordered the corpse to be kept under police surveillance until the burial. Just before the moment of interment, the lid of the tiny coffin was lifted to show the coroner's chief officer that the body of the babe was still present – just in case it had been substituted. Then, and only then, was tiny Lily Evans laid to rest.

THE FINAL REST OF CHIEF LONG WOLF

Sioux Indian Chief Long Wolf died of bronchial pneumonia while appearing with Buffalo Bill's Wild West Show at Earl's Court during its European tour in 1892. Long Wolf's dying wish was to be returned home to native soil for burial. As his wife feared he would be put over the side of the ship and buried at sea, Buffalo Bill Cody saw to it that a respectful burial was made in England. A fine stone memorial was erected in Brompton Cemetery. Over 100 years later, Elizabeth Knight, a Worcestershire housewife, was so moved to read that Long Wolf's grave was laying overgrown and forgotten that she set about tracing his living family and raising the money to have the great chief returned home. With due ceremony and reverence, Long Wolf was exhumed and returned home for interment at the Oglala Sioux burial ground at the Pine Ridge Reservation in September 1997.

THE UNDERTAKER
AND FUNERAL DIRECTOR

Before the nineteenth century funerals for the British general public were normally simple rites governed more by tradition and custom than any notion of solemnity, pomp, 'decency', and due ceremony: it was rare to find a tradesman who made a living as an undertaker. Even in the larger towns and cities those entrusted with carrying out the preparation of the dead for burial would have had other, allied occupations. Tradesmen's sign-boards and plaques in cities frequently announced such combinations as 'Builder and Undertaker'.

Death was, for the Victorians, a fact of everyday life. Many people of influence had been appalled by the drunken revelry which accompanied a pauper's funeral. As a 'middle class' emerged in the nineteenth century a clear move towards moral standards of sobriety, Christian values, manners and education emerged, well evinced in what has been described as the Victorian 'celebration of death': the fall of the 'undertaker sideline' and the rise of 'the funeral director', the man responsible for overseeing the complete funeral process from the construction of coffins through to the carving and erection of marble and stone monumental masonry and headstones. So began a long tradition of undertakers and funeral directors as a specific trade, often handed down from generation to generation over the last 150 years.

A GOOD SEND-OFF

The main focus of the funeral director was on the funeral itself: to see that the rites were ordered correctly, the hearse provided, the mourners had coaches, and that all necessary attendants, pall-bearers and professional mourners (such as mutes, who would often be dumb men in need of work) were in attendance.

Mutes were dressed with silk-covered hats with 'weepers' trailing down the back, with a wide sash draped over their shoulder. They would usher the cortège with their draped wands. With them were occasionally 'feather men', who carried a great plumed canopy of feathers. This has its origin in the plumed helmets carried at the burial of knights, a theme also reflected in the black ostrich plumes worn on the horses pulling the hearse. But all of this pomp did not come cheaply. In the mid-nineteenth century, the complete funeral of a gentleman of standing cost between £200 and £1,000. A person of the middle class was about £60, and tradesmen of 'the better class' about £50. Burial of tradesmen from 'the lowest class' was £10-12; adults from the 'labouring classes' could be 'laid decently for their class' for around £5; and their children's burials cost around 30s. Parents wealthy enough to erect headstones for their children, but not wishing to be too extravagant, would buy one large stone with enough space for future child fatalities, those who could well share the grave in the not-too-distant future.

There was a great feeling, especially among the poorer classes, that though they might have lived on the poverty line, they would see their beloved family members had 'a good send-off'. Even on some of the poorest streets the clatter of a horse-drawn hearse would be known, complete with all the trimmings of pall-bearers, plumed horses and feathermen. Social commentator Mrs Bernard Bosanquet, in her 1899 book *Rich and Poor*, observed: 'The greatest

festival of all is perhaps the funeral… the poverty of the family makes no difference to their eagerness… I have known a woman have a hearse and four horses, and a carriage and pair, for her husband's funeral, and within two weeks apply to the Guardians to feed her children.'

SHROUDS

The earliest form of covering for most bodies for burial was a simple winding sheet of linen, a custom still observed as late as 1818 in Ireland.

For many years, especially in rural Britain, the chosen covering was a woollen shroud: indeed, in 1666 an Act was passed by which only woollen shrouds were permitted for this purpose. The body would be transported to the grave in a wooden 'shell' or coffin, where it would be taken out and buried. Burial in woollen shrouds was still known in country areas as late as the 1880s: one description of the shroud from this period is recorded by Ernest Suffling in *Epitaphia* (1909): 'My own father, who died in 1888, was habited in a pale green-grey flannel shroud finished at the throat, ankles and wrist with cut points. The wrists and ankles of the garment were drawn in tightly with pink flannel and the body tricked out with little cut rosettes of the same.'

THE COFFIN

In country areas the duty of building a coffin mostly fell to the village carpenter or wheelwright, and any burial customs would be carried out by the bereaved family, friends and neighbours from the village. Despite funerals being simple affairs, they still carried a hefty expense for poorer households. To avoid leaving their loved ones with a bill, country folk would often have their coffins made before they died and use them in their cottages as cupboards!

It was not unknown for people to outgrow their coffins, or to use coffins made for others for those who suffered a premature death: a bad fit was often cured by the undertaker breaking the ankles of the deceased. The shroud covered all, so the body appeared to fit well when it was visited while 'lying in' before burial – although the fact that the deceased appeared to be a lot shorter in death than in life did not always pass without comment…

COFFIN OF CHOICE

In the past the finest way to send off your dear-departed was in a wooden coffin with fine brass handles, decorative coffin plates and a black velvet pall. In the modern world the choices are almost limitless. Coffins can be made of material including: recycled newspapers; wool; wickerwork; compressed cardboard with rope handles; a biodegradable plastic liner; there is even a fair-trade coffin made from banana leaves.

The vast array of shapes for coffins now available includes: a canal boat; a skate board; a ballet shoe; a vintage Rolls-Royce car; a Mercedes; a lion; a chicken; a fish; a pineapple; a huge brogue shoe; a Nike trainer shoe; a space rocket; a guitar; an enormous cocoa bean; a hot dog; a pint of beer; a Coca-Cola bottle; a Nintendo entertainment system games controller; a red pillar post box; a train carriage; a handbag; a Nokia mobile phone; a massive Rothman's King Size cigarette; a skip; and a Red Arrows jet aeroplane. There is even a coffin with a built-in computer, complete with keyboard and screen fitted in the lid… just in case, I guess!

COFFINS CAN BE DANGEROUS

Thirty-six-year-old Henry Taylor was one of six pall-bearers carrying a coffin towards its grave at Kensal Green Cemetery, in London, in 1872 when he stumbled and fell to the ground. To the horror of the mourners, the other bearers let go of the coffin and it fell, with great force, onto Taylor's upper body, smashing his jaw and ribs. The funeral carried on as Taylor was removed to University Hospital, where he died from his injuries a few days later.

In a more recent incident, Marciana Silva Barcelos, a passenger in the hearse carrying her husband's coffin on the way to his funeral in Rio Grande do Sul, Brazil, in 2008, met a surprising fate: a speeding Alfa Romeo car crashed into the back of the hearse, catapulting the coffin forward and slamming it into the back of Mrs Barcelos's head, killing her instantly.

THE HEARSE

In the Victorian age the best of funerals saw the deceased, in their coffin, transported in a fine, glass-sided hearse pulled by a magnificent team of black horses decked out with plumes and polished harness. In the twenty-first century a funeral director in Melbourne, Australia, takes it to a new level by offering a limousine-style hearse with room for twelve mourners. The hearse is fitted out with chrome hand-rails, tinted windows, its own mini-bar, DVD player, coffee machine, ambient lighting and pop-out cup holders. Classy.

CREMATION IN HISTORY

Cremation was known to ancient people around the world at least 20,000 years ago and was practiced among the Neolithic, Bronze Age, Iron Age, Ancient Roman and Ancient Greek people.

Cremation fell out of favour in Western civilizations during the Middle Ages, and was forbidden by law in many countries.

In 1658, English physician Sir Thomas Browne advocated cremation as a means of disposing of the human body for the first time in the modern world.

The first recorded cremation in modern Britain took place on 26 September 1769. The body of Honoretta Pratt, the daughter of Sir John Brookes of York, was illegally burned in an open grave at St George's Burial Ground, London, and a stone bearing the following inscription was erected in the burial ground, Hanover Square, London, saying:

> This worthy woman believed that the vapours arising from graves in churchyards in populous cities must prove hurtful to the inhabitants and resolving to extend to future times, as far as she was able, that charity and benevolence which distinguished her through her life, ordered that her body should be burnt in the hope that others would follow the example, a thing too hastily censured by those who did not enquire the motive.

The great strides towards reinstating cremation in the modern world began when Paduan Professor Brunetti presented a cremation chamber at the Vienna Exposition in 1873.

Prominent British surgeon and polymath Sir Henry Thompson attended the Vienna Exposition, where he saw the working model of the cremator designed by Professor Brunetti. Thompson was deeply impressed, returned to Britain and became the leading founder of the Cremation Society of Great Britain when he called a meeting of a number of his friends at his house at 35 Wimpole Street, London, on 13 January, 1874. There the following declaration was drawn up:

> We, the undersigned, disapprove the present custom of burying the dead, and we desire to substitute some mode which shall rapidly resolve the body into its component elements, by a process which cannot offend the living, and shall render the remains perfectly innocuous. Until some better method is devised we desire to adopt that usually known as cremation.

Among the notable signatories were Shirley Brooks, Frederick Lehmann, John Everett Millais, John Tenniel, Anthony Trollope and Sir T. Spencer Wells.

The first custom-built crematorium in the UK was built in Woking, Surrey, in 1878, but local people objected and an appeal to prohibit the use of the building remained in force until 1884.

In 1884, cremation was declared legal after Dr William Price, an eccentric and a practising Druid, attempted to cremate the body of his five-month-old son Iesu Grist (Jesus Christ) in his garden at Llantrisant, Wales. Price was prevented from doing so by a mob of locals, who pulled the body of the babe from the flames. Price was then arrested by the local police for what they believed was the illegal disposal of a corpse. Brought before a court in Cardiff, Price argued that while the law did not state that cremation was legal, it also did not state that it was illegal. The judge, Mr Justice Stephen, agreed. Price was freed, and he was allowed to cremate his child.

The first cremation to take place at Woking Crematorium, and the first official cremation of a person in the UK in modern times, was that of Mrs Jeannette C. Pickersgill on 26 March 1885.

The right for local authorities to establish crematoria was formally established in law under the Cremation Act, 1902.

Under the Cremation Act of 1902, no crematorium could be built closer than 50yds to any public highway, or in the consecrated area of an extant burial ground.

The first crematorium in London was opened at Golders Green in 1902.

Open-air funeral pyres were made illegal in Britain by the 1930 revision of the Cremation Act.

In 1885 there were 597,357 deaths in the UK, but only three persons were cremated. By 2010, however, there were 493,242 deaths registered in England and Wales, and just over 73 per cent of the bodies were cremated.

ALL YOU EVER WANTED TO KNOW ABOUT CREMATION BUT WERE AFRAID TO ASK

In the UK the deceased is cremated with their coffin, which is why all British coffins that are to be used for cremation must be combustible. The Code of Cremation Practice forbids the opening of the coffin once it has arrived at the crematorium, and rules stipulate that it must be cremated within seventy-two hours of the funeral service.

A cremator is an industrial furnace that is able to generate temperatures of 760 to 1,150°C (1,400 to 2,100°F) to ensure disintegration of the corpse.

Coal and coke were originally used to fuel cremators but oil, natural gas and propane are the modern fuels of choice.

No stacking is allowed: indeed, the retorts (the chamber where the body is placed to be cremated) in all cremators are not designed to incinerate more than one body at a time. Most cremators are built to one standard size but most of the larger cities in the UK have access to an oversized cremator that can handle corpses of 200kg (440lb) and above.

The only non-natural item required to be removed from a body in preparation for cremation is a pacemaker, because it could explode and damage the cremator.

The greater portion of the body (especially organs and other soft tissues) is vaporized and oxidized by the intense heat during the cremation process and gases are discharged through the exhaust system. The process usually takes ninety minutes to two hours, but larger bodies take longer.

After the incineration is completed, what are left are not ashes, *per se*, but rather dry bone fragments. These are allowed to cool down; they are then swept out of the retort and removed to a 'cremulator' that pulverises them into 'ashes' by means of a grinder (or heavy metal balls, in older machines). This final process takes around twenty minutes.

The ashes of adults weigh from 4lb (1.8kg) for most women and up to 6lb (2.7kg) for men.

A company in Illinois, USA, offers (for a price) a unique use for the ashes of the dearly departed: they make 'memorial diamonds' from carbon captured during the cremation.

TO GO WITH A BANG

A company in Essex known as 'Heavens Above' offers a service whereby the ashes of the dearly departed are packed into fireworks and let off in displays for family and friends.

A FINAL WISH

Every effort is made to oblige the requests of families for their dearly departed to be cremated in the clothing they would have wanted, mentioned in their will or final wishes. One problem did arise after a Formula One fan asked to be cremated in the racing suit he had been given by one of his racing heroes: it was found to be flame retardant.

DECOMPOSITION

Five stages are generally applied by modern pathologists to describe the process of human decomposition: Fresh, Bloat, Active and Advanced Decay and Dry/Remains.

Fresh: The stage immediately after the heart stops beating. Blood stops circulating and gravitates to the dependant parts of the body where a bluish-purple discolouration, commonly referred to as lividity, can soon be observed. *Rigor mortis*, the stiffening of the muscles, occurs after about three to four hours, reaches maximum stiffness after twelve hours and gradually dissipates over approximately forty-eight to sixty hours.

Bloat: Anaerobic metabolism occurs at this stage, leading to the accumulation of gases within the body cavity which cause an appearance of 'bloating'. As the pressure of the gases within the body increases, fluids are forced to escape from natural orifices, such as the nose, mouth, and anus, and enter the surrounding environment. The build-up of pressure, combined with the loss of integrity of the skin, may also cause the body to rupture. The gases that accumulate within the body at this time aid in the transport of sulfhemoglobin throughout the body via the circulatory and lymphatic systems, giving the body a marbled appearance. If the body is exposed to insects, maggots hatch and begin to feed on the body's tissues at this stage.

Active Decay: Maggots feed voraciously. Liquefaction of tissues and disintegration become apparent during this stage, and strong odours persist. The end of active decay is signalled by the migration of maggots away from the body to pupate.

Advanced Decay: The body is reduced to a carcass, and insect activity reduces dramatically as the cadaveric material is eaten away.

Dry/Remains: All that is left of the cadaver at this stage is dry skin, cartilage, and bones. If all soft tissue is removed from the cadaver, it is termed skeletonised, but if only portions of the bones are exposed, it is referred to as partially skeletonised.

The speed at which decomposition occurs varies greatly. Factors such as temperature, humidity, and the season all determine how fast a fresh body will skeletonise or mummify. The basic guide for the effect of environment on decomposition is known as Casper's Law (or Ratio): if all other factors are equal, then, when there is free access of air, a body decomposes twice as fast than if immersed in water and eight times faster than if buried in earth. Ultimately, the rate of bacterial decomposition acting on the tissue will depend upon the temperature of the surroundings. Colder temperatures decrease the rate of decomposition while warmer temperatures increase it.

14

IN MEMORIAM

IN AFFECTIONATE REMEMBRANCE OF
CHARLES WILLEY,
Who Died December 29th, 1847,
AGED 5 YEARS AND 6 MONTHS;
ALSO OF
WILLIAM THOMAS WILLEY,
Who Died December 29th, 1847,
AGED 3 YEARS AND 1 MONTH;
ALSO OF
WILLIAM WILLEY,
Who Died April 11th, 1850, Aged 4 Months.

Oh, how I loved those darling boys
I hope in heaven to see;
Can I forget their lovely smiles,
Which made them dear to me.

FUNERALIA

The ethos and an industry of 'funeralia' was a typically Victorian enterprise and catered for every possible funeral requisite, from wreaths (artificial and fresh) to black mourning silks for dresses (with Whitby jet jewellery to accompany them). There was even a 'cheaper end of the market' which made gutter percha or vulcanite mourning jewellery and impressed tin plaques and plated metal handles to dignify and decorate the cheaper coffins. Black-edged mourning stationery, known as '*In Memoriam*' cards, also abounded – some with the most intricate and embossed designs, to the degree these cards were frequently mounted in yet further embossed card mounts with weeping angels, willows, dowsed torches and all manner of funeral impedimenta and symbolism. These would be framed in sober black frames, perhaps with a golden border, and hung with pride in sitting rooms.

COMPETITIVE MOURNING

From the *East Suffolk Almanac* in 1885: 'When the mourners all got home Mr Grant tied crape upon all window shutters, to show how deeply he mourned; and as Fisher knew that his grief for Mrs Fisher was deeper, he not only decorated his shutters, but he fixed 5yds of black bombazine on the bell-pull and dressed his whole family in mourning. Then Grant determined that his duty to the departed was not to let himself be beaten by a man who couldn't feel any genuine sorrow, so he sewed a black flag on his lightning rod, and festooned the front of his house with black alpaca. Then Fisher became excited, and he expressed his sense of bereavement by painting his dwelling black, and by putting up a monument to Mrs Fisher in his front yard. Grant thereupon stained his yellow horse with lampblack, tied crape to his cow's horn, daubed his dog with ink and began to wipe his nose on a black handkerchief.'

YOU CAN'T TAKE IT WITH YOU

An inscription in St Michael's churchyard, Macclesfield, illustrates the weakness for the love of display of the poor at a funeral:

MARY BROOMFIELD
dyd 19 Novr., 1755, aged 80.
The chief concern of her life for the last twenty years
was to order and provide for her funeral. Her greatest
pleasure was to think and talk about it. She lived many
years on a pension of ninepence a week, and yet she saved
£5, which, at her own request, was laid out on her funeral.

DEATH AT THE FUNERAL

A terrible tragedy occurred in June at the town of Rovinj on the Istrian Coast of the Adriatic in June 1895. The body of a deceased young man had been placed upon an upper floor in his house and around seventy friends gathered to pay their last respects when the floor of the old building gave way, plunging many of the mourners into a deep cellar – killing fourteen and causing serious injuries to twenty-five.

LIFELIKE AND EVERLASTING

The only life-size wax funerary figure known to survive outside Westminster Abbey in London is that of Sarah Hare, who died on 2 April 1744. Her figure, complete with realistic glass eyes and curly dark hair, is dressed in a fine silk dress and shrouded by a red silk cape and is displayed, in a fine, glass-fronted mahogany case, in the Hare family chapel at Stow Bardolph, in Norfolk.

THE CASTS OF POMPEII

One of the remarkable legacies left by the eruption of the volcano Vesuvius in AD 79 is the number of strangely shaped holes found in the volcanic deposits around Pompeii. These represent the corpses of people and animals killed by the pyroclastic flow and buried by the hot ash. As the ash solidified before the corpses decayed, a 'mould' of Vesuvius's victims was created. Early in the excavation, Giuseppe Fiorelli discovered that filling these moulds with plaster resulted in highly accurate and eerie forms of those who failed to escape. Their last moment of life has thus been captured forever: their postures, and even their expressions (usually of terror), are often clearly visible.

THE CONSTANT GUEST OF THE DUCHESS

The Duchess of Marlborough was so bereft after the death of former lover William Congreve (1670-1729) that she had a life-like wax image of him made and placed at her toilette table. Theophilus Cibber claimed in his *Lives of the Poets of Great Britain and Ireland*, 'To this she would talk as if to the living Congreve, with all the freedom of the most polite and unreserved conversation.'

A UNIQUE MEMORIAL

In the church of Little Parndon, Essex, is a headstone to Hester Woodley, who died in 1767 in her sixty-eighth year. The stone is almost unique in Britain, for it marks the grave of an African woman who was sold into slavery. Hester faithfully served two generations of the Woodley family in the village: when Mrs Bridget, the lady of the house, died, her daughter 'inherited' Hester.

IRON-MAD

John 'Iron-Mad' Wilkinson (1728-1808) was probably the greatest pioneer and promoter of cast iron in the early years of the Industrial Revolution. He was one of the founders of Ironbridge, and in fact produced about one eighth of Britain's total national production of iron in the 1790s. It was during that time his 'iron madness' reached its peak – almost everything around him made of iron. Even when he died he kept true to his beloved iron, having his coffin fashioned in the metal and a massive iron obelisk to mark his grave at Lindale.

KNICKERS FOR BOYS

When the eccentric Revd John Gwyon – rector of St John the Baptist church, Bisley, Surrey, for thirty-three years – took his life on Boxing Day in 1928, he left all of his £9,976 estate to provide knickers for the poor boys of Farnham, with the further stipulation that each garment was to be marked 'Gwyon's Present'.

FILL IN THE GAPS

When Benjamin Smith died at King's Lynn, Norfolk, at the age of ninety-three, in 1829, his gravestone had already been standing in St Margaret's churchyard for nearly ten years: it had blanks ready to be filled in for the day and date of his death.

SMOKING KILLS

Marie Ellis, a lifelong smoker, defied medical logic when she died of heart failure at the age of 105 in December 2004. A smoker since the age of fifteen, she was still smoking fifteen a day when she died. A wreath in the shape of a cigarette was placed on her coffin, and she was cremated clutching a packet of her favourite Benson & Hedges. The old folks' home in Westgate, Kent, where she spent her last years, planned to build a garden memorial to her – in the form of a concrete ashtray.

FLASH, BANG, WALLOP

The Victorians loved the comparatively new art of photography and photographs would be taken by professional photographers at all the key events in life – birth, marriage and even death. Many family albums of the nineteenth century contain morbid pictures of (mostly elderly) departed relatives, although a 'sleeping' bride or baby may not always be what it immediately appears to be. It was very rare that the living were photographed while asleep!

THE MAN WHO 'PHOTOGRAPHED' GHOSTS

The first photographs of 'ghosts' were taken by a man named William H. Mumler (1832-1884), who made his fortune by his discovery.

He was a very competent engraver in the employ of Bigelow of Boston (USA) in 1861. In his spare moments Mumler took to studying photography. The discovery was purely accidental: he had omitted to clean his camera properly, so that two impressions were rendered on one plate, the first less distinct than the second. Mumler was very sharp and did not fail to take advantage of his secret. He succeeded in producing these effects in a permanent way. He left his former profession and set up in business as a spirit photographer.

This is how the business was carried on. The customer who wished to have the photograph of the spirit of a dear one departed had to send his or her cabinet photograph and a fee of twenty francs; then there would be a sitting and, a few days afterwards, the photographs were received: the original image, and the new photograph showing the sitter with the ghost of their loved one. It so happened that a father desired the photo of his dead son's ghost. On receipt of the photos, however, he found that the two-year-old boy's ghost had grown to that of a man of at least thirty.

This mishap, and many others, finally attracted the attention of the authorities and the business was declared illegal in 1875.

A GRAVE FIT FOR AN EXPLORER

When the great Victorian explorer and translator of *The Arabian Nights* Sir Richard Burton died in 1890, his wife Isabel saw to it that a great sandstone mausoleum be erected to his memory in St Mary Magdalene churchyard, Mortlake, London – in the shape of the tent Burton had made for his travels with Isabel in Syria! It is a remarkably beautiful example of stone masonry – it even shows details such as minor creases and tension lines in the 'canvas'. Isabel joined her husband after her death in 1896 and their coffins can still be seen through a window at the back of the monument, surrounded by both Christian and Islamic symbols and grave goods.

A LASTING AND TASTEFUL MEMORIAL

Urns for the retention and display of human ashes can take many forms. Decorative containers can be glass, natural marble, metal or wood. Some companies offer a variety of specialised and novelty-shaped urns. Examples include a wooden urn with a working battery-powered clock on it – ideal for the mantle shelf – or an urn engraved with the badge of the deceased's favourite football club; a camouflage-painted urn; a golf bag and clubs; a mallard duck; a police public call box for the *Dr Who* fan; an urn in the shape of cowboy boots; and even a wall-mounted motorcycle display plaque (where the ashes are placed in a decorated motorcycle petrol tank).

ARTIST IN THE INK

When legendary Marvel comic-book writer Mark E. Gruenwald, the editor, writer and co-writer of so many classic story series over the years (*Spider-Woman*, *Captain America*, *Thor*), passed away in 1996, his final request was that he be cremated and his ashes mixed with the ink used to print the first-run trade-paperback compilation of his *Squadron Supreme* stories. Copies of this particular first edition now (2012) exchange hands for sums in excess of $500.

ASHES TO ASHES, DUST TO BUST

Following on the theme of receptacles for cremated remains, it was reported in a Brisbane newspaper in 2001 that a young Australian widow who had lost her husband in a car accident wanted some of her late husband's ashes to be injected into her breast implants so he could always be close to her heart.

HE HAS BOLDLY GONE

When James Doohan, the original 'Scotty' in the TV series *Star Trek*, passed away in 2005 his last wish was that some of his ashes should go into space – and so they did, along with those of 200 others, aboard the *SpaceLoft XL* in 2007. The rocket entered outer space in a four-minute suborbital flight and then returned to earth, as planned, with the ashes still inside. Doohan's ashes were then sent up in *Falcon 1* in 2008, but this rocket malfunctioned (perhaps because it just 'didnae have the power'). Finally, in May 2012, a small urn containing his remains was flown into space aboard the *Dragon* spacecraft.

THE LONDON NECROPOLIS

By the mid-nineteenth century the churchyards of London were many feet deep with centuries of burials. Increasing concerns and official enquiries into the health of the capital led to the creation of The London Necropolis and National Mausoleum Co., established by Act of Parliament in 1852. Two thousand acres of common land at Woking were purchased from Lord Onslow and laid out as Brookwood Cemetery. The proud boast of the Necropolis was that it was 'large enough to contain all of London's dead for ever.' When Brookwood opened in 1854 it was the largest cemetery in the world. Because it was situated 25 miles outside the city, a direct rail link was constructed to the cemetery: The Necropolis Light Railway. It had a private terminus near Waterloo Station. At the cemetery there were two stations – one for Anglicans, the other of nonconformists. Class distinctions were also observed and three classes of tickets (first, second and third) were available for both passengers and coffins – although the latter were only sold as singles!

15

STRANGE
EPITAPHS

'Let's talk of graves, of worms, and epitaphs.'
Shakespeare – *Richard II*, Act 3, Scene 2

Horatio Norfolk, William Andrews and Ernest Suffling published three of the greatest British compilations of epitaphs in the nineteenth and early twentieth centuries: *Norfolk's Gleanings from Graveyards* (1861), Andrew's *Curious Epitaphs* (1883) and Suffling's *Epitaphia* (1909). Although full details are not always recorded, they assured their readers that, to the best of their belief, the epitaph did exist at the time and had, in many instances, been collected by worthy academic gentlemen and the authors themselves.

The following is a selection of favourites, with the addition of many epitaphs collected by the author from a number of Victorian epitaph collectors' manuscripts, notebooks that survive in private and public collections, his own archive and the many graveyards he has visited over the years.

In June 1767, John Catchpole, a wagoner of Palgrave in Suffolk, reaching the great age of seventy-five, set out on one last trip to see the sights of London, the scene of his weekly peregrinations as a younger man. Horses and man in need of refreshment, he pulled up at a public house in Sudbury. As the ostler was removing the horses' bridles they bolted, overturning the cart – with John Catchpole still aboard. Terribly bruised, the poor old wagoner died the next day. John was given a fine tombstone in Palgrave churchyard with the epitaph:

My horses have done running,
My wagon is decay'd
And now in the Dust my body is lay'd
My whip is worn & and my work It is done
And now I'm brought here to my last home.

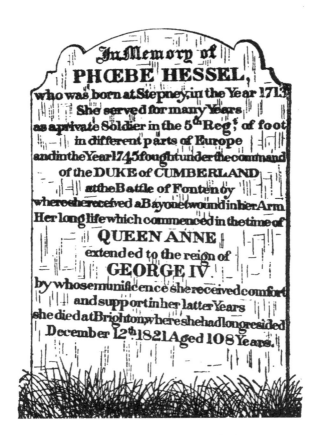

In Memory of
PHŒBE HESSEL,
who was born at Stepney, in the Year 1713.
She served for many Years
as a private Soldier in the 5th Regt of foot
in different parts of Europe
and in the Year 1745 fought under the command
of the DUKE of CUMBERLAND
at the Battle of Fontenoy
where she received a Bayonet wound in her Arm.
Her long life which commenced in the time of
QUEEN ANNE
extended to the reign of
GEORGE IV.
by whose munificence she received comfort
and support in her latter Years
she died at Brighton where she had long resided
December 12th 1821 Aged 108 Years.

On Sam Cook, Belchamp Walter, Essex, who died in May 1800, aged eighty-nine years:

Snug by the wall lies old SAM COOK
Who with his Spade, his Bell and Book
Serv'd Sexton three Score Years and Three
Until his Master, grim death, cry'd
Enough, your tools now lay aside
And let a Brother bury thee.

The headstone of William Simonds, who died at Woodditton, Cambridgeshire, on 1 March 1757, at the age of eighty, bears a grill at the top of the stone. Behind this is his iron dish. The inscription reads:

Here lies my corpse, who was the man,
That lov'd a sop in dripping pan.
But now believe me I am dead,
Now here the pan stands at my head.
Still for sop to the last I cry'd,
But could not eat and so I died.
My neighbours they perhaps may laugh,
Now they do read my epitaph.

SOME BRITISH EPITATHS

Here lies father, and mother, and sister, and I.
We all died within the space of one year,
They all be buried at Whimble except I,
And I be buried here.

(From Edworth, in Bedfordshire)

I would have my neighbours all kind and mild,
Quiet and civil to my dear wife and child.

(The grave of Robert Loder in Marston, Bedfordshire)

Here lies a fair blossom, moud'ring to dust,
Ascending to heaven, to dwell with the just.

(Swallowfield, Berkshire)

When this you see remember me
As I lay under ground,
The world say what it will of me
Speak of me as you have found.

(Allworth Chapel, Windsor, Berkshire)

Once at his death, and twice in wedlock blest;
Thrice happy in his labour and his rest;
Espoused now to Christ, his head in life,
Being twice a husband, and in death a wife.

(On William Hawkins at Iver, Buckinghamshire)

An honest man, a friend sincere,
What more can be said? He's buried here.

(On Richard Carter, Iver, Buckinghamshire)

Here lies the body of Mary Gwynne,
Who was so very pure within,
She cracked the shell of earthly sin
And hatched herself a cherubim!

(Cambridge)

Beneath this stone lyes Edward Green,
Who for cutting stone famous was seen.
But he was sent to apprehend
One Joseph Clarke, of Kerredge End,
For stealing Deer of Squire Dounes,
Where he was shot, and died o'th wounds.

(Prestbury, Cheshire)

On an old woman who sold pots:
Beneath this stone lies Cath'rine Gray,
Changed to a lifeless lump of clay.
By earth and clay she got her pelf,
Yet now she's turn'd to Earth herself.
Ye weeping friends let me advise,
Abate your grief, and dry your eyes.
For what avails a flood of tears?
Who knows, but in a run of years,
In some tall pitcher or broad pan,
She in her shop may be again?

(Chester, Cheshire)

There lies entomb'd within this vault so dark,
A Tailor, cloth draw'r, soldier, and a clerk.
Death snatch'd him hence, and also from him took
His needle, thimble, sword, and prayer book.
He could not work nor fight, what then?
He left the world, and faintly cry'd – Amen.

(St John's church, Chester)

Reader, take notice,
That on ye 12 Feby 1760,
Tho: Corbishley,
A brave veteran Dragoon
Here went into his quarters.
But remember that when
The trumpet calls
He'll out and march again.

(Gawsworth, Cheshire)

Here lies entombed one Roger Morton,
Whose sudden death was early brought on;
Trying one day his corn to mow off,
The razor slipped and cut his toe off:
The toe, or rather what it grew to,
An inflammation quickly flew to;
The parts they took to mortifying,
And poor dear Roger took to dying.

(Acton, Cornwall)

Old Doll Pentreath, one hundred age and two,
Both born and in Paul parish buried too;
Not in the church 'mongst people great and high,
But in the church-yard doth old Dolly lie!
  (On Dolly Pentreath, St Paul's churchyard, Mousehole, Cornwall)

Here lies the body of Joan Carthew,
Born at St Columb, died at St Cue,
Children she had five,
Three are dead, and two alive,
Those that are dead chusing rather
To die with their Mother, than live with their Father.

(St Agnes, Cornwall)

Here lies we
Babies three,
Here we must lie
Until the Lord do cry,
'Come out, and, live wi' I!

(Truro, Cornwall)

Tis my request
My bones may rest
Within this chest
Without molest
(George Warrington, died 1727, St Stephen's, Dunheved, Cornwall)

Here lies, in a horizontal position,
the outside case of
George Routleigh, Watchmaker,
whose abilities in that line were an honour to his
profession.
Integrity was the mainspring, and prudence the regulator
of all the actions of his life;

Humane, generous, and liberal, his hand never stopped
till he had relieved distress:
So nicely regulated was his movements,
that he never went wrong,
except when set a-going
by people who did not know his key:
Even then he was easily set right again.
He had the art of disposing of his Time,
so well,
That his hours glided away in one
continual round of pleasure and delight,
Till an unlucky moment put a period to his existence.
He departed this life November 14, 1802,
aged 57, wound up,
in hopes of being taken in hand by his Maker:
and of being thoroughly cleaned, repaired, and set a-going
for the world to come.

(Lydford, Devonshire)

Here lie I, at the Chancel door;
Here I lie, because I'm poor;
The further in, the more to pay;
Here I lie as warm as they!
  (On a man who was too poor to be buried with his relations in the
                                church, Kingsbridge, Devonshire)

Joan was buried the 1st day of Feby. 1681.
Bartholomew was buried the 12th day of Feby. 1681.
She first deceas'd – he a little try'd
To live without her – lik'd it not, and died.
  (Bartholomew Doidge and Joan, his wife, Milton Abbot, Devonshire)

Here lie the remains of James Pady, Brickmaker, late of the parish,
In hopes that his clay will be remoulded in a workmanlike manner,
far superior to his former perishable materials.

(Unknown location)

Keep death and Judgement always in your eye,
Or else the devil off with you will fly,
And in his kiln with brimstone ever fry.
If you neglect the narrow road to seek,
Christ will reject you, like a half Burnt Brick.

(Awliscombe, Devon, John Linning, 1824)

Stop, reader! stop and view this stone,
And ponder well where I am gone.
Then, pondering, take thou home this rhyme –
The grave next opened may be thine.

(Maker, Devon)

THE BLIND AND GOOD EARL

On the tomb of Edward Courtenay, 3rd Earl of Devon, commonly called 'the blind and good Earl', an epitaph, frequently quoted, appears. The Earl died in 1419, and his Countess was Maud, daughter of Lord Camoys. He is buried in Tiverton, Devon.

Hoe! hoe! who lies here?
I, the goode Erle of Devonshire;
With Maud, my wife, to me full dere,
We lyved togeather fyfty-fyve yere.
What wee gave, wee have;
Whatt wee spent wee had;
What wee left, we loste.

On Robert Trollop, architect of the Exchange and Town Court of Newcastle:

Here lies Robert Trollop,
Who made yon stones roll up:
When death took his soul up,
His body filled this hole up.

(Gateshead, Tyne & Wear)

Martha Blewitt of the Swan, Baythorn-End,
of this Parish,
buried May 7th, 1681.
Was the wife of nine Husbands
successively, but the 9th outlived her.
The Text to her Funeral Sermon was:—
'Last of all the Woman died also.'

(Chelmsford, Essex)

Here lies poor Charlotte,
Who died no harlot;
But in her virginity,
Of the age nineteen,

In this vicinity,
Rare to be found or seen.

(Bristol)

Here lies the Earl of Suffolk's fool,
Men call'd him Dicky Pearce,
His folly serv'd to make folks laugh,
When wit and mirth were scarce.
Poor Dick, alas! is dead and gone!
What signifies to cry?
Dickeys enough are still behind,
To laugh at by and by.
Buried 1728.

(Berkeley, Gloucestershire)

Here lies I and my two daughters,
Killed by drinking Cheltenham waters;
If we had stuck to Epsom salts,
We shouldn't be lying in these here vaults.

(Cheltenham, Gloucestershire)

Our bodies are like shoes, which off we cast,—
Physic their coblers, and Death their last.

(Cirencester, Gloucestershire)

On John Buckett, Landlord of the King's Head Inn, who died on 2 November 1802:

And is, alas! Poor Buckett gone?
Farewell, convivial, honest John.
Oft at the well, by fatal stroke,
Buckets, like pitchers, must be broke.
In this same motley shifting scene,
How various have thy fortunes been!
Now lifted high - now sinking low.
To-day thy brim would overflow,
Thy bounty then would all supply,
To fill and drink, and leave thee dry;
To-morrow sunk as in a well,
Content, unseen, with truth to dwell:
But high or low, or wet or dry,
No rotten stave could malice spy.
Then rise, immortal Buckett, rise,
And claim thy station in the skies;

'Twixt Amphora and Pisces shine,
Still guarding Stockbridge with thy sign.

(Stockbridge, Hampshire)

In memory of
THOMAS THATCHER
a Grenadier in the North Regiment of Hants Militia,
Who died of a violent fever contracted by drinking small beer when hot
The 12th of May 1764, aged 26 years.
Here sleeps in peace a Hampshire grenadier,
Who caught his death by drinking cold small beer;
Soldiers beware, from his untimely fall,
And, when you're hot, drink strong, or none at all.

When the above stone, in Winchester, Hampshire, was restored by the
officers of the garrison in 1781 they added the comment: 'An honest
soldier is never forgot, Whether he die by musket or by pot.'

This Stone
was erected by the
Brethren
of Lodge CXI. of
Free and accepted
Masons,
As a token of respect
for their departed
Brother,
Jonathan Triggs,
who received a
Summons
From the Great Architect
Of the Universe,
At the hour of High Twelve,
on the 24 day of October.
A.L. 5819.
A.D. 1819.
Aged 38 years.

(Winchester Cathedral churchyard)

When I am dead and in my Grave,
And all my Bones are Rotten.
This when you see, Remember me,
Or lest I should be forgotten.
(On Hannah, wife of Jeremiah Soffe, died 1832: Ryde, Isle of Wight)

Here a lovely youth doth lie,
Which by accident did die;
His precious breath was forced to yield,
For by a waggon he was killed!

(Hereford, Herefordshire)

Captain Henry Graves, died 17th Aug. 1702,
Aged 52 years.
Here, in one Grave, more than one Grave lies—
Envious Death at last hath gained his prize;
No pills or potions could make Death tarry,
Resolved he was to fetch away Old Harry.
Ye foolish doctors, could you all miscarry?
Great were his actions on the boisterous waves,
Resistless seas could never conquer Graves.
Ah! Colchester, lament his overthow,
Unhappily, you lost him at a blow;
Each marine hero for him shed a tear,
St Margaret's, too, in this must have a share.

(Hoddeston, Herefordshire)

Here lyes the Conqueror conquered,
Valient as ever England bred;
Whom neither art, nor steel, nor strength,
Could e'er subdue, till death at length
Threw him on his back, and here he lyes,
In hopes hereafter to arise.

(On a Wrestler: Bluntisham, Huntingdonshire)

Sixteen years a Maiden,
One twelve Months a Wife,
One half hour a Mother,
And then I lost my Life.

(Folkestone, Kent)

Though young she was,
Her youth could not withstand,
Nor her protect from Death's
Impartial hand.
Like a cobweb, be we e'er so gay,
And death a broom,
That sweeps us all away.

(Rochester, Kent)

Grim death took me without any warning
I was well at night, and died in the morning.

(Sevenoaks, Kent)

Mary Hill, died 1784.
With pain and sickness wasted to a bone,
Long time to gracious Heaven I made my moan;
Then God at length to my complaint gave ear,
And sent kind Death to ease my pain and care.
Physicians could no longer save the life
Of a tender mother and a loving wife.

(Harby, Leicestershire)

To a sailor:
My helm was gone,
My sails were rent,
My mast went by the board,
My hull it struck upon a rock,
Receive my soul, O Lord!

(Horncastle, Lincolnshire)

Of tender threads this mortal web is made,
The woof and warf, and colours early fade;
When pow'r divine awakes the sleeping dust,
He gives immortal garments to the just.

(On Henry Fox, a weaver, Sleaford, Lincolnshire)

This tombstone is a Milestone.
Hah! How so?

In Affectionate Remembrance
OF
P.C. Stephens,
Who passed away on April 4th, 1908,
Aged 48 years.

He did 22 years' Service on the Leicester Police Force,
and was acknowledged to be England's Heaviest
Constable, his weight being over 24 stone.
He also served his Country in the Zulu War, 1879.

Poor old Stephens, how we'll miss him
From his customary beat;
Never more his stalwart figure
Or stern, but kindly face we'll greet!

"REQUIESCAT IN PACE."

Because, beneth lies Miles,
Who is Miles below.

(Tombstone of John Miles, Welby, Lincolnshire)

Reader pause. Deposited beneath are the remains of
Sarah Biffin,
who was born without arms or hands, at Quantox Head,
County of Somerset, 25th of October, 1784, died at
Liverpool, 2nd October, 1850. Few have passed through
the vale of life so much the child of hapless fortune as the
deceased: and yet possessor of mental endowments of no
ordinary kind. Gifted with singular talents as an Artist,
thousands have been gratified with the able productions
of her pencil! whilst versatile conversation and agreeable
manners elicited the admiration of all. This tribute to
one so universally admired is paid by those who were best
acquainted with the character it so briefly portrays.

(St James's Cemetery, Liverpool)

He sang the Song of the Shirt.

(Poet Thomas Hood, died 1845, Highgate Cemetery, London)

Praises on tombs are vainly spent:
A good name is a monument.

(On Jean Anderson, died 1770, Hammersmith, London)

Here lie the Quick and the dead.

(On William Quick, Kensal Green Cemetery, London)

A peerless matron, pride of female life,
In every state, as widow, maid, or wife;
Who, wedded to threescore, preserv'd her fame,
She lived a phœnix, and expired in flame

(On Lady Molesworth, who died in a fire, Islington, London)

Here lies Dame Dorothy Peg,
Who never had issue except in her leg,
So great was her art, and so deep was her cunning,
Whilst one leg stood still the other kept running.

(St Dunstan, London)

F. Barlow ad vivum delin.

P. Tempest sc.

THE
Robin-Red-Breast
Famous for singing every day on the Top of QUEEN
MARY's Mausoleum Erected in Westm.r Abbey 1695

Be silent every Grove and Plaine,
And listen to my sweeter Straine.
Your Choristers can neither Vie
With Me in Theam, nor Harmony.
You, Nature's Blooming Beauties sing,
But, I The Godess of the Spring.
Your Scene are Silvan Bowrs, but Mine
A Temple, and MARIA's Shrine,
Your Song may Nimphs, and Shepheards warme,
But Mine th's Saints, and Angels Charme.

VERY STATE

A CURIOUS ACROSTIC

Here Sept. 9th, 1680,

WAS BURIED

A True Born Englishman,
Who, in Berkshire, was well known
To love his country's freedom 'bove his own:
But being immured full twenty years
Had time to write, as doth appears —

HIS EPITAPH.

H ere or elsewhere (all's one to you or me)
E arth, Air, or Water gripes my ghostly dust,
N one knows how soon to be by fire set free;
R eader, if you an old try'd rule will trust,
Y ou'll gladly do and suffer what you must.
M y time was spent in serving you and you,
A nd death's my pay, it seems, and welcome too;
R evenge destroying but itself, while I
T o birds of prey leave my old cage and fly;
E xamples preach to the eye — care then (mine says),
N ot how you end, but how you spend your days.

(Chepstow, Monmouthshire)

Some have children, some have none,
Here lies the mother of twenty-one.

(Anne Jennings, Wolstanton, Newcastle-under-Lyme)

When on this spot affection's downcast eye,
The lucid tribute shall no more bestow;
When friendship's breast no more shall heave a sigh
In kind remembrance of the dust below;

Should the rude sexton digging near this tomb,
A place of rest for others to prepare,
The vault beneath to violate presume,
May some opposing Christian cry 'Forbear' —

Forbear! rash mortal, as thou hop'st to rest
When death shall lodge thee in thy destined bed,

With ruthless spade, unkindly to molest
The peaceful slumbers of the kindred dead.

(A tomb in Norfolk)

Alas! alas! Will. Scrivenor's dead, who by his art,
Could make Death's Skeleton edible in each part.
Mourn, squeamish Stomachs, and ye curious Palates,
You've lost your dainty Dishes and your Salades:
Mourn for yourselves, but not for him i' th' least.
He's gone to taste of a more Heav'nly Feast.

(William Scrivenor, cook to the Corporation, died 1684. St
Margaret's, King's Lynn, Norfolk)

All you that do this place pass bye
Remember death for you must dye.
As you are now even so was I.
And as I am so that you be.
Thomas Gooding here do staye
Wayting for Gods judgement daye

(Norwich Cathedral, Norfolk)

Here lies John Racket
In his wooden jacket,
He kept neither horses nor mules;
He lived like a hog,
He died like a dog,
And left all his money to fools.

(Woodton, Norfolk)

On William Brown, died 1863
Reader, pass on, nor spend your time
On bad biography, nor on bitter rhyme;
For what I was this lump of clay ensures,
And what I am is no affair of yours.

(Honing, Norfolk)

Here lies doomed,
In this vault so dark,
A soldier, weaver, angler and clerk;
Death snatched him hence, and from him took
His gun, his shuttle, fish-rod and hook.
He could not weave, nor fish, nor fight, so then
He left the world, and faintly cried - Amen.

(Great Yarmouth, Norfolk)

Time flies away as nature on its wing,
I in a battle died (not for my King).
Words with my brother soldier did take place,
Which shameful is, and always brings disgrace.
Think not the worse of him who doth remain,
For he as well as I might have been slain.

(On George Griffiths of the Shropshire Militia, who died as
a result of fighting with a brother soldier, 26 February 1807, Great
Yarmouth, Norfolk)

This monumental stone records the name
Of her who perished in the night by flame
Sudden and awful, for her hoary head;
She was brought here to sleep amongst the dead.
Her loving husband strove to damp the flame
Till he was nearly sacrificed the same,
Her sleeping dust, tho' by thee rudely trod,
Proclaims aloud, prepare to meet thy God.

(Elizabeth Cliff, who died in 1835, Burton Joyce, Nottinghamshire)

Does worm eat Worm? Knight Worme this truth confirms,
For here, with worms, lies Worme, a dish for worms.
Does worm eat Worme? sure Worme will this deny,
For Worme with worms, a dish for worms don't lie.
'Tis so, and 'tis not so, for free from worms,
'Tis certain Worme is blest without his worms.

> (On Sir Richard Worme, Peterborough Cathedral)

Many years I've seen, and
Many things I have known,
Five Kings, two Queens,
And a Usurper on the throne;
But now lie sleeping in the dust
As you, dear reader, shortly must.

> (On Rowland Deakin, died 1791, aged ninety-five. Astley
> churchyard. Shrewsbury, Shropshire)

Stephen and Time
Are now both even;
Stephen beat Time,
Now Time beats Stephen.

> (On 'little Stephen', a noted fiddler, Hadleigh, Suffolk)

Here lies Jane Kitchen, who, when her glass was spent,
Kickt up her heels, and away she went.

> (Bury St Edmunds, Suffolk)

As I walked by myself, I talked to myself,
And thus myself said to me:
Look to thyself, and take care of thyself,
For nobody cares for thee.
So I turned to myself, and I answered myself,
In the selfsame reverie,
Look to myself, or look not to myself
The selfsame thing it will be.

> (On Robert Pycroft, died 1810, aged ninety; Homersfield, Suffolk)

To the Memory of
THOMAS TIPPER who
Departed this life May the 14th
1785 Aged 54 Years.
READER, with kind regard this GRAVE survey
Nor heedless pass where TIPPER'S ashes lay,
Honest he was, ingenuous, blunt, and kind;

And dared do, what few dare do, speak his mind,
PHILOSOPHY and HISTORY well he knew,
Was versed in PHYSICK and in Surgery too,
The best old STINGO he both brewed and sold,
Nor did one knavish act to get his Gold.
He played through Life a varied comic part,
And knew immortal HUDIBRAS by heart.
READER, in real truth, such was the Man,
Be better, wiser, laugh more if you can.

(On the grave of Tomas Tipper, a brewer, Newhaven, Sussex)

As a warning to female virtue,
And a humble monument of female chastity,
This stone marks the grave of
Mary Ashford,
Who, in the 20th year of her age, having
Incautiously repaired to a scene of amusement,
Was brutally violated and murdered
On the 27th of May, 1817.
Lovely and chaste as the primrose pale,
Rifled of virgin sweetness by the gale,
Mary! the wretch who thee remorseless slew
Avenging wrath, who sleeps not, will pursue;
For though the deed of blood was veiled in night,
Will not the Judge of all mankind do right?
Fair blighted flower, the muse that weeps thy doom,
Rears o'er thy murdered form this warning tomb.

(Sutton Coldfield, Warwickshire. Ashford's brother refused to fight
the man who he believed had killed Mary, the last time that the
defence of 'trial by battle' was used in an English courtroom)

Here lies the bones, of Joseph Jones,
Who ate whilst he was able;
But once o'erfed, he drop't down dead
And fell beneath the table.
When from the tomb, to meet his doom,
He rises amidst sinners;
Since he must dwell, in heav'n or hell,
Take him – which gives best dinners.

(On Joseph Jones, died 1690, Wolverhampton)

ROBERT BURNS ON DEATH

No lesser man than Robert Burns is said to have written the following epitaph for innkeeper John Dove:

Here lies Johnny Pigeon:
What was his religion?
Whae'er desires to ken,
To some other warl'
Maun follow the carl,
For here Johnny had none!
Strong ale was ablution -
Small beer persecution,
A dram was memento mori:
But a full flowing bowl
Was the saving of his soul,
And port was celestial glory.
(Mauchline, East Ayrshire)

Here lies John Taggart, of honest fame,
Of stature low, and a leg lame;
Content he was with portion small,
Kept a shop in Wigtown, and that's all.
        (On shopkeeper John Taggart, Wigtown, Galloway, Scotland)

Stop, passenger, until my life you read,
The living may get knowledge from the dead:
Five times five years I lived a virgin life,
Five times five years I was a virtuous wife,
Five times five years a widow, grave and chaste,
Tired of the elements, I am now at rest;
Betwixt my cradle and my grave were seen
Eight mighty Kings of Scotland and a Queen;
Thrice did I see old Pulacy pulled down,
And thrice the cloak did sink beneath the gown.
                (On Margery Scott, Dunkeld, Perthshire, Scotland)

Sacred to the memory of a character,
John Cameron, `Johnnie Laddie,'
A native of Cambeltown, Ardersier,
Who died there August 26, 1858, aged 65 years.
Erected to his memory by public subscription.
Sixty winters on the street,
No shoes nor stockings on his feet;

Amusement both to small and great,
Was poor `Johnnie Laddie.'

(Brachlach, Scotland)

My engine now is cold and still,
No water does my boiler fill;
My coke affords its flame no more;
My days of usefulness are o'er;
My wheels deny their noted speed,
No more my guiding hand they need;
My whistle, too, has lost its tone,
Its shrill and thrilling sounds are gone;
My valves are now thrown open wide;
My flanges all refuse to guide,
My clacks also, though once so strong,
Refuse to aid the busy throng:
No more I feel each urging breath';
My steam is now condensed in death.
Life's railway o'er, each station's passed,
In death I'm stopped, and rest at last.
Farewell, dear friends, and cease to weep:
In Christ I'm safe; in Him I sleep.
(On a steam engine driver, died 1840, Bromsgrove, Worcestershire)

Nigh to the river Ouse, in York's fair city,
Unto this pretty maid death shew'd no pity;
As soon as she'd her pail with water fill'd
Came sudden death, and life like water spill'd
   (On the loss of a sweetheart in December 1796, her lover wrote,
                                                    York, Yorkshire)

John Gray
In the sixteenth year of his age, on the night of January
19th, 1858, was swept by the fury of a storm, from the
pierhead, into the sea. We never found him — he was
not, for God took him; the waves bore him to the hollow
of the Father's hand. With hope and joy we cherished
our last surviving flower, but the wind passed over it, and
it was gone.

(Holy Trinity church, Hull, Yorkshire)

In memory of
John, the son of John and
Ann Bywater, died 25th January,

1815, aged 14 years.
Life's like an Inn, where Travellers stay,
Some only breakfast and away;
Others to dinner stay and are full fed;
The oldest only sup and go to bed;
Long is the bill who lingers out the day,
Who goes the soonest has the least to pay.

(Hull, Yorkshire)

Here lies the body of William Stratton, of Paddington,
Buried 18th day of May, 1734, aged 97 years;
Who had by his first wife 28 children;
By his second 17;
Was own father to 45;
Grandfather to 86;
great Grandfather to 23.
In all 154 children.

(Hyden, Yorkshire)

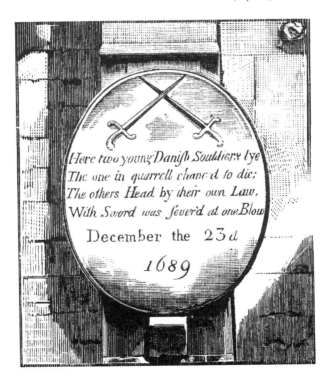

Here two young Danish Souldiers lye
The one in quarrell chanc'd to die;
The others Head by their own Law,
With Sword was sever'd at one Blow

December the 23d

1689

On the body of John Moore, murdered in 1750:
Unto the mournful fate of young John Moore,
Who fell a victim to some villain's power;
In Richmond Lane, near to Ask Hall, 'tis said,
There was his life most cruelly betray'd.
Shot with a gun, by some abandon'd rake,
Then knock'd o' th' head with a hedging stake,
His soul, I trust, is with the blest above,
There to enjoy eternal rest and love;
Then let us pray his murderer to discover,
That he to justice may be brought over
(Richmondshire, North Yorkshire)

BURIED UPRIGHT

When Ursula Hewytt, of Breckles, Norfolk, died, her will of 1674 (proved in 1678) requested she be buried in an upright position. Her round black ledger slab in the chancel bears the inscription STAT UT VIXIT ERECTA – 'as upright in death as she was in life'.

THE SUICIDE'S GRAVE

At the time that Elizabeth James of Peterborough took her own life with poison, suicides could not be interred in consecrated ground and thus she was buried in the road leading to Spalding. The relations of the unfortunate girl erected a stone nearby inscribed:

Near this spot were deposited, on 24th May 1811, the sad remains of Elizabeth James; an awful momento against the horrid crime of suicide – Passenger! Take warning: you see here a fatal instance of human weakness and the dreadful consequence of misplaced affection.

THE BLACKSMITH'S EPITAPH

This fine verse can be found on many memorial stones of blacksmiths across Britain:

My Sledge and hammer lie reclined,
My Bellows, too, have lost their wind;
My fire's extinct, my forge decayed,

And in the dust my vice is laid;
My coal is spent, my iron gone,
My nails are drove, my work is done.

THE APOPLEPTICK DART

Bridgett Applethwaite's ledger stone in Bramfield church, Suffolk, states:

After the fatigues of a married life bravely born by her with Incredible Patience for four years and three quarters bating three weeks; and after the Enjoiment of the Glorious Freedom of an Easy and Unblemish't widowhood, for four years and upwards, She resolved to run the risk of a second Marriage-bed. But DEATH forbade the banns, and having with an Apopleptick dart (the same instrument with which he had formerly dispatch't her Mother) Touch't the most vital part of her brain. She must have fallen Directly to the ground (as one Thunder-strook) if she had not been catch't and supported by her Intended Husband. Of which invisible bruise, after a Struggle for above sixty hours, with that Grand Enemy of Life (but the certain and Merciful Friend to Helpless Old Age) In Terrible Convulsions, Plaintive Groans or Stupefying Sleep, without recovery of her speech or senses, She dyed on ye 12th day of September in ye year of Our Lord 1737 and of her own Age 44.

THE RIDDLE OF TOM OTTER

Ten tongues in one head,
Nine living and one dead.
One flew forth to fetch some bread
To feed the living in the dead
The answer? It's the Tom Tit that built in Tommy Otter's head.

To make more sense of this rhyme, the reader should be aware that Tom Otter's body was gibbeted after his execution for the murder of his newlywed wife Mary Kirkham near Saxilby in Lincolnshire in 1806.

ACKNOWLEDGEMENTS

Any attempt at a bibliography for this book would result in a very unwieldy list of publications, but the author would like to extend his thanks to his team of experts and friends who have made suggestions for subjects and facts to research and include, helped check facts and endured my obsession with, and excitement for, the strange and the obscure:

Andrew Selwyn-Crome; Ian Pycroft; Kitty Jones; Stewart P. Evans; Major Graham Bandy; Janet McBride; James Nice; Martin Sercombe; Britta Pollmuller; Martin and Pip Faulks; Rebecca Matthews; Kerry and Paul Nicholls; Dr Stephen Cherry; Dr Vic Morgan; the late Theo Fanthorpe; Lionel Fanthorpe; Robert 'Bookman' Wright; Sarah Stockdale; Helen Radlett-Henry; Michael Howroyd; Robert Bell; Julia and Nigel Gant; Jenny Phillips; Sophie Dunn; Michelle Bullivant; Steve and Eve Bacon; Victoria Barrett; Christine and David Parmenter; Ted Round; the late John Timpson; my mother Diane; my darling Molly and son Lawrence.

If you enjoyed this book, you may also be interested in…

Little Book of Great Britain

NEIL R. STOREY

This little gem of a book is a repository of intriguing, fascinating, obscure, strange and entertaining facts and trivia about Britain and the things that have made it great – inventors and inventions, manners and customs, great Britons, great places (castles, cathedrals, notable buildings, museums, collections and national parks), and the best of British music, food and sports.

978 0 7524 7114 3

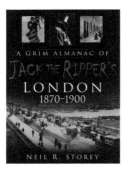

A Grim Almanac of Jack the Ripper's London, 1870-1900

NEIL R. STOREY

Jostling for position in this cornucopia of the criminal and the curious are tales of baby farmers, garrotters, murderers, poisoners, prostitutes, pimps, rioters and rebels. This colourful cast of characters is accompanied by accounts of prisons and punishments, executions and disasters. If it's horrible or strange, then it's here!

978 0 7509 4859 3

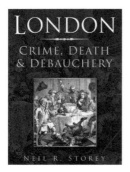

London: Crime, Death & Debauchery

NEIL R. STOREY

Featuring countless stories of infamous misdeeds and scandalous behaviour, the book includes duelling, murder, gaol breaks, rioting, body-snatchers, robbery, suicide, drinking, infanticide, gambling, highwaymen, fraud and executions. Illustrated with a series of engravings, drawings and photographs that help to paint a picture of historic London's seedier side, Neil R. Storey brings together a selection of tales to shock, scare and entertain.

978 0 7509 4624 7

Visit our website and discover thousands of other History Press books.

www.thehistorypress.co.uk